"Verne Harnish's Mastering the Rockefeller Habits *is clearly the most important management tool that we have implemented. It has created clarity and focus throughout our organization. These tools have helped our management deal with the elephants instead of the ants and lead us to become an* INC. 500 *company."*

DWIGHT COOPER, PRESIDENT, PPR TRAVEL
JACKSONVILLE BEACH, FLORIDA

"Verne's principles have had a dramatic positive impact on our company. Over the past three years his tools have helped propel our company to the Inc. 500 *list (# 17)."*

MARK HOLLAND, PRESIDENT AND CEO, ASCEND HR SOLUTION
SALT LAKE CITY, UTAH

"Verne is the backbone of this country's entrepreneurial community. His advice and wisdom have influenced more rapid growth companies than anyone I know. This book is a MUST BUY for companies facing the challenges of business growth—be prepared to pull it off your shelf often."

ANDREW J. SHERMAN, SENIOR PARTNER, MCDEMOTT, WILL & EMERY;
AUTHOR OF 11 BOOKS ON THE LEGAL AND STRATEGIC ASPECTS OF BUSINESS GROWTH
WASHINGTON, D.C.

"There are few people who have had the wealth and range of experience of Verne Harnish in terms of observing and assisting rapidly growing and entrepreneurially managed enterprises. Verne's presentation skills, in conjunction with his ever-expanding knowledge base, permit him to communicate useful ideas regarding the management of growth-focused businesses in an effective and memorable manner. Those reading Verne's writings are likely to become enriched as a result."

ARTHUR LIPPER, FORMERLY EDITOR-IN-CHIEF, *VENTURE* MAGAZINE
SAN DIEGO, CALIFORNIA

"I LOVE your book. I've written all over it, learned a GREAT deal from it, and won't lend it to anyone (but I'll buy them a copy). One of my favorite sections is 'Short and Sweet' on page 'xx' of the Introduction. I agree with every word. Your book packs more intellectual firepower into less space than just about ANY book I can recall."

ERIC LEE SMITH, FOUNDER, GIVINGCAPITAL, INC.
PHILADELPHIA, PENNSYLVANIA

"I have integrated these principles into my organization and as a result we have significantly strengthened our contribution to our employees, clients, investors, and community. The bonus is that I have become a better leader too."

CYNTHIA B. KAYE, PRESIDENT & CEO, LOGICAL CHOICE TECHNOLOGIES, INC.
DULUTH, GEORGIA

"The Rockefeller Habits are so simple yet so powerful in their application. Our company has become more focused, informed and coordinated to achieve our most important objectives." DAMON GERSH, PRESIDENT & CEO, MAXONS RESTORATIONS, INC.
NEW YORK, NEW YORK

"Business management is a vastly complex undertaking. Harnish's tools, methodologies and simple truisms (like 'Doing the Right Things Right') help eliminate what can be the blinding complexities, and in turn bring clarity to the process of aligning, and better managing the business enterprise."
MARK D. GORDON, CHIEF ENERGIZING OFFICER, SYNERGY NETWORKS, INC.
VIENNA, VIRGINIA

"Verne's tools helped me more than any other business educational tool I have ever used. In just a few short days of exposure to his teaching, I was able to go home and begin a revolution that would prove to change our company for the better for the balance of time."
BILL HUDSON JR., CEO, HUDSON SALVAGE INC.
HATTIESBURG, MISSISSIPPI

"Verne Harnish supplies the mental tools to grow and prosper—I am living proof."
RUSSELL VAIL, PRESIDENT, CLEARSAIL COMMUNICATIONS, LLC
HOUSTON, TEXAS

"This is very powerful stuff! If you don't believe me, ask any one on my management team."
ROB SOLOMON, CHAIRMAN, USOL HOLDINGS, INC.
AUSTIN, TEXAS

"Not only have we used the principles in our business but we have also applied them in our consulting practice to our clients—prioritization is so powerful."
DARRYL DEMOS, CEO, DEMOS CONSULTING GROUP
NORWELL, MASSACHUSETTS

"I understood I had a lot to learn before I met Verne, I just didn't realize my lack of knowledge was so vast. Verne's lessons have made significant improvements in my organization. My people are happier, my clients express greater satisfaction, my profits are improving and we have implemented structure to a formerly entrepreneurial seat of the pants organization."
ERICK W. SLABAUGH, CEO, ABSCO ALARMS, INC.
EDMONDS, WASHINGTON

"Verne Harnish taught me a lot of valuable things that I was able to apply in my four companies. At the beginning of this year we for example started with daily huddles in our companies. I am very happy with the results. Verne Harnish doesn't teach boring academic theories— he teaches us things we can immediately put into practice to make our companies more successful."
ALEX S. RUSCH, RUSCH PUBLISHING
SWITZERLAND

"After spending a few days with Verne, I was able to positively change the way I viewed business, customers and employees, and that proved to be the missing link in the development of our business."
NOEL J. GUILLAMA, CHAIRMAN & CEO, TARGITINTERACTIVE, INC.
PORTSMOUTH, NEW HAMPSHIRE

"Verne has developed tools and techniques to help create global leaders in every field. He pushes the entrepreneur towards corporate greatness."

RICHARD P KIVEL, CEO, MOLECULARWARE, INC
CAMBRIDGE, MASSACHUSETTS

"His book is essential reading for anyone looking to benchmark best industry practices that generations of entrepreneurs have been using. It unlocks the secrets compiled from the lessons (and mistakes) of this country's most successful entrepreneurs."

LARRY CHIANG, CEO & FOUNDER, UNITED COLLEGE MARKETING SERVICES;
AND AUTHOR OF *INTERNET MARKETING SECRETS*

"By staying focused on the Rockefeller Habits we were able to align our organization and focus on what counts before getting lost in the details. It has become part of our Operating Handbook."

MARK T. ANDERSON, CEO, ANDERSON HAY & GRAIN CO., INC.
ELLENSBURG, WASHINGTON

"Verne has made a career of learning what successful people do to make companies grow. The things he teaches are simple solutions to complex business problems that really work. He taught us some great techniques for focusing and aligning our efforts that have had immediate impact on our productivity."

DAVID HALL, PRINCIPAL, SEARCHCONNECTION
COLUMBIA, MARYLAND

"I can attribute a great deal of my success to what I learned from Verne Harnish. The programs created by Verne, have not only impacted how I manage my personal life and business, but have also opened a door to an international group of business owners that I now actively use as my outside board of directors and advisors on tough critical issues. The lessons combined with the relationships fostered by Verne have provided the education and confidence for me to grow my company to $20 million in just three years."

CHARLES G. HALL IV, PRESIDENT, CHARLES HALL CONSTRUCTION
CLARENDON HILLS, ILLINOIS

"To grow and lead a successful business, I recognize the need for professional and business development activities. I have met many business consultants and regularly attend many leadership programs. Verne's advice and guidance, stands out from the pack. In this book Verne provides the most potent, practical insight and direction necessary for growing a business with focus, accountability and rhythm."

RICHARD M. BRUEGGMAN, DATA SCIENCE AUTOMATION, INC.
CANONSBURG, PENNSYLVANIA

"With this material we redefined our market niche through a uniquely sustainable competitive advantage and grew our revenue over 50% in the first year of implementation."

JEFF STEPLER, PRESIDENT, TELCOM TRAINING CORPORATION
IRVING, TEXAS

"Working with companies like AOL, NBC, Gateway, sophisticated investors and others, it has become clear to me that execution is the most critical strategic weapon. Verne has been instrumental in mastering and transferring the visionary and executionary tools and habits that have allowed my companies to succeed where others have failed. A database is nothing without an effective execution plan."
GREGORY CARSON, CEO, CITL, INC.
NEW YORK, NEW YORK

"We have begun to make many of the changes that I learned from Verne. We did the whole planning pyramid and 45 days later the 400 plus employees can now recite what the key measure are and what our brand promise is. Even more impressive is that people are behaving differently. It is so simple it is beautiful!"
JOHN STEPLETON, PRESIDENT, RESEARCH DATA DESIGN, INC.

"Many companies suffer from their inability to benchmark. Verne's business fundamentals helped us to learn to benchmark while understanding where to buy the lumber and make it square. We've been sitting pretty ever since!"
MAURICE GLAVIN, TOTAL SCOPE, INC.
BOORWYN, PENNSYLVANIA

"Verne's work allowed us to focus and articulate our vision and plans for the company. We struggled for months to get our hands around the project. Verne's tools assisted us in pulling together the strategic plan of TimeVision in a concise, understandable format. Now we can spend the time executing and not struggling with definitions."
LOIS MELBOURNE, PRESIDENT & CEO, TIMEVISION, INC.
IRVING, TEXAS

"As a CEO of a fast growth company (four year rate 871%), finding the one "choke point" has allowed us to focus the whole company on maximizing our competitive advantage. Thanks to Verne, we should be growing at four digits in the coming year."
SAMUEL CHANG, CEO, WISDOM CLOTHING COMPANY
DULLES, VIRGINIA

"Verne is an outstanding student of business, and his abundant findings frequently translate into business initiatives for our company."
TIM HANDLEY, CHAIRMAN & CEO, ADVANTAGE COMPANIES

"When growing a profitable company seems its most demanding and complex, Verne is a master of providing simple tools to make it all seem possible and a lot easier to accomplish."
JEFF FREEMYER, CEO, CONVERGENT MEDIA SYSTEMS
ATLANTA, GEORGIA

"Verne's enterprise building tools helped create controls that identified large holes in our systems and procedures. Once identified, we saved millions annually and the savings continue to multiply today."
HAROLD SOLOMON, SERAPHIM PARTNERS, LLC
ATLANTA, GEORGIA

"Verne Harnish's toolbox for businesses provided our company the keys to building a solid team in a fast growth environment, which enabled us to jump to the front of the line in our marketplace. His leadership has inspired entrepreneurs throughout the world and the results have been immeasurable!"

MICHAEL J MALONE, CHAIRMAN & CEO, MJM INVESTIGATIONS, INC.
MORRISVILLE, NORTH CAROLINA

"Verne Harnish is without doubt the clearest thinker in entrepreneurial education and development today."

SCOTT TANNAS, CADVISION
CALGARY, ALBERTA

"Our daily five-minute huddles have been going on now for two years. The huddle provides the opportunity to report critical numbers that affect the overall goals and objectives of our company while fostering rhythm, alignment and team building of our employees. Before implementing our five-minute huddles our monthly meetings would last over five hours, now it's down to 90 minutes."

MICHAEL CABRERA, PRESIDENT & CEO, ANCICARE PPO, INC.
MIRAMAR, FLORIDA

"Verne fostered an environment that encouraged entrepreneurism with discipline, which has been highly effective for my company."

DEVIN SCHAIN, CEO, ON CAMPUS MARKETING
BETHESDA, MARYLAND

"Learning from Verne how to Master the Rockefeller Habits propelled my company farther ahead in one week than we had moved the entire past year. We never used to have scheduled meetings. Using the Rockefeller Habits to establish a meeting rhythm really aligned our management team. Now we can't live without our daily huddle and weekly 'Hour of Power.'"

ROGER SCHEUMANN, PRESIDENT & OWNER, QUARTERMAINE COFFEE ROASTERS
ROCKVILLE, MARYLAND

"These tools helped me set goals for the organization and then meet them, for example, make the Inc. 500, raise capital to scale the company, and once funded, open multiple centers to be better poised for acquisition."

JEANNE LAMBERT, PRESIDENT & CEO, CERIDA CORPORATION
ANDOVER, MASSACHUSETTS

"Verne is the master of 'actionable' tools. His practical advice has helped align our firm around what's important and energized our team to reach for what they thought was impossible. Verne himself is a gazelle among gazelles."

JOHN WARRILLOW, PRESIDENT, WARRILLOW & CO., INC.
TORONTO, ONTARIO

"Verne is able to put into words some of things that are hard to express but you know are just good common sense when it comes to business. His presentations and tools have helped me communicate these ideas more effectively throughout my organization."

JOHN SCIARABBA, ALDEN SYSTEMS

"Verne reveals the dos and don'ts of growing a business. We know better what to do as we grow, because of the lessons learned from others' mistakes and successes."
JOEL STEVENS, PC OUTLET INC. AND PC OUTLET LLC
RICHMOND HILL, ONTARIO

"I was amazed by what kinds of effects a few simple ideas, consistently applied, can have on my company. We are now much more focused, our goals and objectives are clearer, and you might even argue that our management team and staff efforts are aligned!"
JEFF BEHRENS, PRESIDENT, THE TELLURIDE GROUP, INC.
NEWTON, MASSACHUSETTS

"We are on course for an 86% increase in net profit, thanks to Verne Harnish's training."
THOMAS P. RIETZ, PRESIDENT & CEO, CANTERRA HOMES, INC.
SCOTTSDALE, ARIZONA

"Verne Harnish has made a huge difference in our company by shaping our strategic direction. He helped our leadership see the big picture of the business environment and greatly expand our horizon."
PETER PHILLIPS, PRESIDENT, THE PHILLIPS GROUP
MIDDLETOWN, PENNSYLVANIA

"Verne Harnish is a visionary. His work inspired me to listen to my inner wisdom and helped me to develop the habits and skills to support success in every area of my life."
MARLA DURDEN, PROFOUND HARVEST, INC.
SEATTLE, WASHINGTON

"Within one week of implementing these tools I felt dramatic effects! It was quite amazing how everything crystallized within a few months. Our clients even began to comment on the success of our consultants and the new level of servicing we were able to offer. I have told many others about these wonderful tools who have since implemented them and found staggering results. It is almost impossible to imagine running a business without them."
KRISTINE DOYLE, MAVEN, INC.
NEW YORK, NEW YORK

"Verne's dissection of business dynamics allows you to reduce your list of 100 'To Do's that you will never get done, down to one or two that your can actually accomplish and have an incredible impact."
GARY M. COONAN, PRESIDENT & CEO, STINGER INDUSTRIES, LLC
MURFREESBORO, TENNESSEE

"Verne Harnish's insights are captivating on the theoretical level and, more importantly, the tools he has developed for implementation have proven very practical and effective for our company."
DAVE P. LIMA, CEO, BEST UPON REQUEST
CINCINNATI, OHIO

"With all the challenges of driving a rapidly growing global business, the alignment we have created between our international offices by utilizing the Rockefeller Habits has been hugely successful."
BRYAN HANSEL, CEO, V I R D E V
EAGAN, MINNESOTA

"It was because of what I learned from Verne that I was able to catch an embezzlement that was going on in my office that not even my CPA caught! Thanks Verne. You never know when all your tips will come to use; you saved my business!" ALISON BIERHOFF, CEO & OWNER, EXCLUSIVE DESIGNS NEW YORK, INC NEW YORK, NEW YORK

"Since I met Verne, I always want to hear more from him. His enthusiasm and communication skills made it fun and easy for a non English-speaking person to grasp everything." ERNESTO ZACHRISSON, ALMO GUATAMELA

"Verne's book equipped me with cogent concepts that helped me to structure my company's "big picture," practical tools that I could apply to real business problems, and inspiration that I could draw on when all else failed. By alerting me to the pitfalls that so many entrepreneurs fall prey to, Verne assured that I would have a business to which I could apply his ideas. I feel the book is an invaluable tool, especially for companies that are new or still evolving." RINA YASUDA, INSYGHT INTERACTIVE, INC. BEVERLY HILLS, CALIFORNIA

"Verne's material allows the business owner to focus on their business as a tool for creating wealth versus a job for a lifestyle. His vision and philosophy allow the entrepreneur to decide if their business is designed and prepared for growth or should just stay where it is. Verne's thoughts have been instrumental in my subsequent business development." STEPHEN H. WATKINS LIGHTHOUSE POINT, FLORIDA

"Getting our company into the rhythm of meetings has helped us focus on what's important and is a major factor in our current growth. Thanks to Verne for sharing this simple yet crucial component to growing a business." REID FUJITA, CEO, RFJO CORPORATION HONOLULU, HAWAII

"We implemented many of Verne's recommendations, which have given us the structure to bring about rapid changes in our organization. These changes have resulted in very profitable growth for our firm." BRAD CRANDALL, JR., E.B. STONE & SON, INC. SUISUN CITY, CALIFORNIA

"Verne's teaching has been very impactful as the execution of his lessons have dramatically increased the success of our organization as we move through storming periods of growth!" DAVE BOULANGER, PRESIDENT, CEO, SUPPLIERPIPELINE INC.

"I never would have gotten to this place in my lifetime without Verne Harnish. The things we shared and put into action have allowed me to accomplish dreams I would not have thought possible." SCOT R. LUND, CEO, ROBERT CARTER CO. OAK PARK, MICHIGAN

MASTERING THE ROCKEFELLER HABITS

What You Must Do to Increase the Value of Your Growing Firm

Verne Harnish

Gazelles Inc.
Ashburn, Virginia

ACKNOWLEDGMENTS

To my children, Cameron, Cole and Jade,
who are helping me rediscover fundamentals,
and to my wife Julie, who supports us all.

A lifetime surrounded by business owners has shaped the thoughts in this book, starting with both my grandparents who each had their own small businesses and my father, a partner in a successful firm for years that collapsed within months when a major customer's funds were frozen by a government agency, leaving dad's firm without the "oxygen" it needed to continue its rapid growth.

Along the way, key business mentors continued to share their wisdom, including Bill Woods, the late Don Simpson, Willard Garvey, and Fran Jabara, the founder of the Center for Entrepreneurship at Wichita State University. It was through my association with Fran that I was exposed to the business savvy of George Ablah, Dan Carney, Frank Carney, Jack DeBoer, Tom Devlin, Larry Jones, Charles Koch, and other highly visible and successful Wichita entrepreneurs and business leaders.

Since then, I must acknowledge the thousands of entrepreneurs that have participated in the Association of Collegiate Entrepreneurs, Young Entrepreneurs Organization, and MIT/Inc./YEO "Birthing of Giants" executive programs. I'll always remember those early annual and highly instructive presentations by Michael Dell and the moving presentation by Steve Jobs, as he described the creation of Apple and his subsequent firing, in front of over 1100 students and young entrepreneurs from around the world. Key business mentors during this time included Arthur Lipper (Arthur continues his active involvement on Gazelles' advisory board) and Bernie Goldhirsh, founders of two of the most important publications of the entrepreneurship movement, and Dr. Warren Winstead and Dr. Rudy Lamone who guided the building of the Young Entrepreneurs Organization and supported my teaching at the University of Maryland.

Special acknowledgement must go to those that have invested in our work at Gazelles including Nick Alexos, Jamie Coulter, Ted Leonsis, John Street, and Alan Trefler and to our board of advisors including Boyd Clarke, John Cone, Tom Delaney, Dan Garner, Howard Getson, Gene Kirila, Andrew Sherman, and Bob Verdun. In addition, several business thought leaders have contributed their thinking and have been ongoing faculty members for the MIT program and/or Gazelles' Master of Business Dynamics program including Dr. Ed Roberts, Dr. Vince Fulmer, Dr. John van Maanen, Dr. Bill Isaacs, Dr. Barbara Bund, Dr. Barrie Greiff, Dr. Neil Churchill, Jack Stack, Don Peppers, Martha Rogers, Jim Kouzes, George Naddaff, Gary Hirshberg, Aubrey Daniels, Randy Fields, Jimmy Calano, Geoff Smart, Duane Boyce, Jack Little, Stuart Moore, and Pat Lencioni. And I've always gained practical business insights from the work of Steve Mariotti and his National Foundation for Teaching Entrepreneurship.

This book would not have been possible without the help and support of the Gazelles' team which included Nicole Pascale, Rob Main, and Blanca Dec. Thanks also to Cindy Anderson who loaned a copy of and encouraged me to read *Titan,* the biography of John D. Rockefeller. And there is always an important and patient team that makes the actual book possible including Ellen Wojahn, who helped with the writing of the Mightwords articles that led to this book. Many thanks to the SelectBook's team which include Dana Isaacson, editor; Nancy Sugihara, copyeditor; Kathleen Isaksen, text design and layout; and Kenzi Sugihara, publisher. They were assisted by Elizabeth Coffee of Bookwrights.com, who handled the cover design, and Mayapriva Long of Bookwrights.com, who handled the cover art direction. And a final thanks to my literary agent, advisory board member, and good friend, Bill Gladstone, of Waterside Productions, who made this book ultimately happen.

CONTENTS

INTRODUCTION:

"HOW-TO" VERSUS "THEORETICAL"

Many business authors write a theoretical book and then hear from their readers: "But how do I implement this stuff?" I chose to do the opposite and write a "how to" book first. After spending twenty years working with and around entrepreneurs, what I've learned CEOs and executives of growing firms want are ideas and tools they can implement immediately to improve some aspect of their business.

Tools that Effect Change

The term "tools" is a deliberate label and comes from a favorite Buckminster Fuller quote that embodies our change management philosophy, "If you want to teach people a new way of thinking, don't bother trying to teach them. Instead, give them a tool, the use of which will lead to new ways of thinking." The tools you are about to learn will effect real and positive changes on your business.

Real and Immediate Results—Why Believe?

Yet why believe these tools are useful? At the front of this book are over 100 CEO endorsements for the tools you'll be acquiring in this book. These are just some of the hundreds of CEOs of mid-size firms that have put our tools to work. We know how important authentic references are to the leaders of mid-size firms. You need to know that what you're going to spend your time learning and implementing actually works in real companies like yours.

Short and Sweet

Like this introduction, I'll not waste a lot of words. The material is structured so you can scan it quickly, pick-up the ideas that matter, and have worksheets you can use to implement those ideas. Except for Chapter 1, which provides an example-rich overview of the application of our tools, the rest of the chapters are structured into bite-sized chunks of information with a liberal use of subheadings and summaries. Enjoy your exploration of these tools.

Weekly Musings

If you like the style and substance of the book, you can receive a very concise weekly email of best practices for managing a growing firm — ideas I pick up each week from executives like you. Each weekly email starts with a short HEADLINE section providing a one to two sentence summary of the main ideas, followed by a DETAILS section providing more specifics for those who wish to dive more deeply into the material. Simply send an email to: vharnish@gazelles.com and put "weekly emails" in the subject line. We'll add you to our growing list of executives.

OVERVIEW

*(Reading this chapter provides a summary
for those executives that want to just scan
the rest of the book)*

What is the underlying handful of fundamentals that drive
everything else that's important in business? What is still fundamental today in building a successful firm that hasn't changed for
over a hundred years? Let me triangulate my answer while providing
an overview of the book's key concepts.

Tom Meredith, former CFO of Dell Computer, and I were discussing how the fundamentals in creating a great business are the
same for parenting great kids. Early in his career before Dell, his wife
had encouraged him to attend a Parent Effectiveness Training (PET)
program. Reluctantly, he attended. However, what he discovered were
some fundamentals that were just as applicable in business as at
home—so much so that he purchased copies for all the executives
where he worked.

Anyone with children will recognize the fundamentals I've summarized as:

1. Have a handful of rules
2. Repeat yourself a lot
3. Act consistently with those rules (which is why you better have
   only a few rules).

About the time my first son was born, as I was studying up on parenting, the book *Titan* was published. More than a biography of John
D. Rockefeller, it detailed many of Rockefeller's leadership and management principles. In fact, it's a must-read for anyone serious in building a successful company. What the book did was confirm three underlying habits I have observed are key to the successful management of a
business and provide what I hope is a catchy label for those habits:

Priorities—Does the organization have objective Top 5 priorities for the year and the quarter (the month if growing over 100% annually) and a clear Top 1 priority along with an appropriate Theme? Does everyone in the organization have their own handful of priorities that align with the company's priorities?

Data—Does the organization have sufficient data on a daily and weekly basis to provide insight into how the organization is running and what the market is demanding? Does everyone in the organization have at least one key daily or weekly metric driving his or her performance?

Rhythm—Does the organization have an effective rhythm of daily, weekly, monthly, quarterly, and annual meetings to maintain alignment and drive accountability? Are the meetings well run and useful?

Titan also confirmed that there is only one underlying strategy—what can be called the "x" factor—which must be discovered, defined, and acted upon to create significant value and ultimately significant valuations within a business:

The "x" factor: identify the chokepoint in your business model and industry and then gain control of that chokepoint.

For Rockefeller, the key to winning in the oil business was gaining an advantage in transportation costs, which is why he was heavily involved with the railroads. Even what appeared to be minor decisions aligned with his focus on transportation costs. When he decided to vertically integrate further by producing his own oak barrels, rather than bring in green timber like his competitors, he had the oak sawed in the woods then kiln dried, reducing their weight and slicing transportation costs in half.

To finish the triangulation, I had the opportunity to spend some time with Steve Kerr, former head of GE's famous Crotonville executive education center. I came away from that meeting with three keys to GE's success that are useful to mid-size firms:

1. In planning, the "middle" is gone. You only have to define two points: where you plan to be 10 to 25 years from now and what you have to do in the next 90 days. The latter point requires real time data and an executive team that can face the brutal reality of what the data is saying and then act accordingly. You don't want to fall in love with your own one to three year plans.
2. Keep everything stupidly simple. If your strategies, plans, decisions, systems, etc. seem complicated, they are probably wrong.

3. The best data is firsthand data. It's why the entire executive team of GE comes to Crotonville each month to "teach." Hanging out with GE managers from around the world along with key customers (letting customers attend Crotonville sessions is key to GE's value proposition) lets the top executives find out what is really going on. It circles back to point #1 and the importance of real time data.

And aligning with the importance of having only a few priorities, Jack Welch, the retired CEO of GE, had only four #1 priorities the entire two decades he was GE's leader.

To illustrate the first GE fundamental I listed above; let me relate a couple decisions made by well-known entrepreneurs. Bill Gates, over twenty years ago, set a very simple company vision—a computer on every desk and in every home. Only recently did Gates and Steve Ballmer, the new CEO of Microsoft, feel that this vision was so close to coming true that it was time to come up with a new one: empower people through great software—any time, any place and on any device. Not particularly fancy, but it's a stake in the ground that is long term.

In parallel, Tom Siebel, founder and CEO of Siebel Systems, has all employees outline their handful of objectives each quarter and post them on an internal portal for everyone to see. (Tom is the first to post and lets all employees see his priorities.) This makes it crystal clear what is expected each quarter, with compensation tied to the quantifiable objectives.

Defining a simple long-term vision 10–25 years out and deciding on a handful of priorities for the next quarter are the two most important decisions a business leader makes. And it's this yin and yang of having both a long-term "rarely changes" piece along side a short-term "changes a lot" dynamic piece that provides the delicate balance needed to drive superior performance.

One last concept and then I'm ready to summarize this overview and give you a quick glance at each chapter. One of our content partners in our Master of Business Dynamics program for senior executives is Strategos, the firm of the great business strategist Gary Hamel (among other things, he's the guru behind the notion of core competencies). The people at Strategos provide a stupidly simple definition of strategy, which I'll paraphrase:

You don't have a real strategy if it doesn't pass these two tests: that what you're planning to do really matters to your existing and potential customers; and second, it differentiates you from your competition.

Add to this the requirement that you have the ability to become the best at implementing this strategy (back to core competencies) and you have a clear idea whether you really have a strategy or not that will work. Some firms do things that differentiate themselves but it doesn't really matter to a customer (high quality when the customer just wants speed) while other firms do things that the customer desires, but so does all the competition (you've just entered the commodity zone). And yet others might have both parts of the strategy correct from a theoretical standpoint, but fail to execute. Keep this simple definition of strategy in mind as you read the rest of the book.

If we now go back and look at the three sets of fundamentals outlined in this overview, we find they integrate nicely (and the rest of the book provides the "how to" for doing this):

1. **Priorities**—there are a handful of rules, some of which don't change much like the core values of the firm and the long-term Big Hairy Audacious Goal (BHAG) and others that change every quarter and every week, what I call the Top 5 and Top 1 of 5. It's the balance of short term and long term.

2. **Data**—in order to know if you're acting consistent to your priorities you need feedback in terms of real time data. There are key metrics within the business that you want to measure over an extended period of time, called Smart Numbers; and there are metrics that provide a short-term laser focus on an aspect of the business or someone's job called a Critical Number. It's the balance of short term and long term.

3. **Rhythm**—until your people are "mocking" you, you've not repeated your message enough. A well-organized set of daily, weekly, monthly, quarterly and annual meetings keep everyone aligned and accountable. And the agendas for each provide the necessary balance between the short term and long term.

What this book will do is provide you some tools for making these simple decisions and then give you the tools for keeping everyone aligned and accountable to those decisions. More specifically:

CHAPTER 1: Written differently than all the other chapters (it became an article in the September 2001 issue of *Fortune Small Business),* it provides a dynamic look at the three barriers to growing a firm and the outcomes you can expect if you implement the three Rockefeller Habits. The second half of the chapter provides a straightforward explanation of the three barriers to growth.

CHAPTER 2: The Right People Doing the Right Things Right model provides an overall framework for what decisions need to be made and in what order to increase the value of your business. It aligns nicely with Jim Collins new research in what it takes to make a good firm great.

Priorities Section

CHAPTER 3: Mastering the One-Page Strategic Plan helps you get your long term and short-term vision, metrics, and priorities on a single page to aid communication and alignment.

CHAPTER 4: Mastering the Use of Core Values provides a way to keep those "rarely changed" handful of rules alive in the company

CHAPTER 5: Mastering Organizational Alignment and Focus gets specific about the Top 5 and Top 1 of 5 approach to prioritization.

CHAPTER 6: Mastering the Quarterly Theme shows how to place a spotlight on the number one priority to keep it top of mind. Dell Computer does this so well.

Data Section

CHAPTER 7: Mastering Employee Feedback provides a process for getting the real time data needed to be "right" about what your priorities should be and to let you know you're acting consistent to those priorities. At the end of the chapter, a brief overview of Smart Numbers and Critical Numbers will be provided.

Rhythm Section

CHAPTER 8: Mastering the Daily and Weekly Executive Meeting provides specific agendas for making these vital meetings effective. Reread the various CEO endorsements if you don't think these meetings are crucial. And at the end of the chapter, a quick overview of the monthly, quarterly, and annual meetings will be provided.

"X" Factor Section

CHAPTER 9: Mastering the Brand Promise provides a simple formula for narrowing in on the key strategy necessary to dominate your market.

Bank Financing Section

CHAPTER 10: Mastering the Art of Bank Financing was co-authored with Rich Russakoff. Rich, without a question, is the best in putting together a loan package that gets banks bidding for your business.

Ten Case Studies

APPENDIX: Please DO NOT overlook the Appendix section—some of the best material, like in Jack Welch's latest book, is in the Appendix. Ten firms are highlighted detailing their specific applications of the tools in the book—along with the results they've achieved. And the case studies are rich with marketing, branding, management, and leadership best practices you can apply in your business.

Implementation

Most of the executives tell us the best way to implement the tools is to purchase a book for every executive and manager and simply go through one chapter per month and discuss how the concepts can be applied to your firm. And several executives are purchasing a book for every employee. It's very inexpensive training and provides the rest of the employees with some important context for the changes management are making. It just makes it easier to get buy-in and gain momentum. You can purchase 20 copies or more for $16.95 each or 50 copies or more for $14.45 each plus shipping. Just go to www.gazelles.com and click on the picture of the book to order.

Electronic Forms

Electronic versions of the various paper forms I highlight throughout the book (like the One-Page Strategic Plan document) are free for you to download at www.gazelles.com—the link is next to the picture of the book you see on the homepage of our site.

Keep on learning and growing!
Verne Harnish, CEO
Gazelles, Inc.
"Increasing the Value of Growing Firms"
vharnish@gazelles.com

1

MASTERING GROWTH

*What CEOs of growing companies know
that you don't—and how you can use it to
build a powerhouse business*

Executive Summary: There are three barriers to growth common among all growing firms: the need for the executive team to grow as leaders in their abilities to delegate and predict; the need for systems and structures to handle the complexity that comes with growth; and the need to navigate the increasingly tricky market dynamics that mark arrival in a larger marketplace. This chapter provides the outcomes you can expect if you implement the three Rockefeller Habits.

Back in 1999, Alan Rudy was a disillusioned CEO. "Wasn't I supposed to be making more money and having more fun, the bigger the company got?" wondered the founder of Express-Med, a mail-order medical supplies firm based in New Albany, Ohio. "I was angry all of the time," remembers Rudy. "I had a long weekend planned to go skiing with my father and two brothers, for the first time in ten years, yet I bagged out at the last minute because the business needed me to hold things together." To make matters worse, on March 30 of that year he was shown financials by his CFO that estimated a first-quarter profit of $300K, yet two days later, on April 1, his CFO said that they had actually *lost* $350K. Chuckles Rudy today, "For several hours, I thought it was an elaborate April Fool's joke. I kept trying to be a good sport about it, yet it turned out to be true." Capping it off during that time were employees in fistfights in the

1

parking lot, and one employee slashing the tires of another because of something said at work. Needless to say "stress was a little high," says Rudy. Yet, within two years Rudy had reversed the trends and his seven-year-old firm has become a $65-million winner. More importantly "It's fun again and we're making money."

Express-Med is among the elite: of all firms in the United States, only 4 percent survive the transition from a small business to a growing firm. David Birch, founder of Cognetics and the official keeper of business growth statistics, calls that 4% "gazelles," which are firms that grow at least 20% a year for four years in a row. These are not huge, old elephants that are cutting back on employees. Nor are they mice—too tiny to create more than a handful of jobs. North America's gazelles—all of which started as mere mice—now fuel more than two-thirds of the continent's economic growth and essentially all of its job creation.

As the statistics indicate, becoming a gazelle isn't easy, requiring the entrepreneur to navigate a specific set of challenges, any one of them potentially life-threatening to the business. The good news is that the barriers to growth are known, and the tools for handling them are within the grasp of any entrepreneur. All it takes to make growing your business both fun and profitable, at each and every stage of its life, is the discipline to find the right tools and implement them.

No one has learned this better than Molly Bolanos. In 1987, Bolanos had in mind a little muffin company; a bakery-and-delivery business that would cater to offices in downtown Seattle. She was 21 and fresh out of college. Bolanos had majored in business, and Mostly Muffins was to be "kind of a case study" to see if she and a partner could pool their savings and start a company. The startup took four years to hit $1 million in revenue. Then the coffee craze hit.

Today Mostly Muffins sells 50,000–60,000 items a day, through Starbuck's, on airlines and Amtrak, at transit stations, and most recently, in grocery stores and food warehouses. The company is on track to hit $10 million in revenue this year. In the midst of tremendous growth and expansion, the company has managed to add six percentage points to its gross margin, while also doubling its cash and tripling the industry average for profits, by following a few business fundamentals outlined throughout this chapter. And Molly herself is in full bloom as a CEO. "I've got my head up and my eyes looking around for opportunity," she says, with satisfaction. "I think $30 million would be great for us."

Though many might consider Bolanos lucky to have ridden the wave of the high-priced coffee craze, the facts are that she and her partner made specific and careful choices along the way, the same choices you must make if you choose to grow your business. "I've found that the stages of growth and the issues you face in a company and as a CEO are very predictable," says Bolanos. "It's positively textbook."

The "textbook" she's referring to are the three fundamental barriers to growth outlined in this book that are common among all growing firms: the need for the executive team to grow as leaders in their abilities to delegate and predict; the need for systems and structures to handle the complexity that comes with growth; and the need to navigate the increasingly tricky market dynamics that mark arrival in a larger marketplace.

Delegating to Others

Most entrepreneurs actually don't like working with anyone, including their own employees! This is the major reason why 96% of all firms have fewer than ten employees, and a vast majority have fewer than three. Therefore, the decision to grow isn't an easy one.

Texan Doug Harrison, CEO of a nearly $200 million provider of mobility aids for the disabled called The Scooter Store, clearly recalls the shift in thinking that brought his business out of a storefront and up to speed. "I remember like it was yesterday the meeting where we decided to grow...in the Sunshine Room of the local Holiday Inn." "We had spent several years struggling to make just our local operation work. We knew our systems weren't ready and we knew growing the business would take us away from our families. But we also knew, once we started making a small profit, that we had a business that could grow," says Harrison. Helping that decision was the threat that came from one of Harrison's so-called friends who saw the same opportunities and became a potential competitor. It was time to bring on more talent.

"One of the first real management concepts that stuck in my head," Harrison says, "was that if you can't afford the people to run the business for you, then all you have is a job, not a business. It was like somebody turning on the light for me, because I realized that I needed to get good people in here to do this for me. I couldn't keep hiring people at as close to minimum wage as possible." Although friends and family were telling Harrison it was too soon to shell out big salaries for experienced sales, operations, and financial people, he did it early in his operation and never looked back. "We went from two locations to five that year, yet we felt we were in better control of the business."

Delegation is just as crucial as the management thinkers have claimed. Harrison knew it was crazy that he was the one deciding whether the bathroom towels would be plain white or blue-striped. And, as a former petroleum engineer, he couldn't pretend to have expertise in finance or sales. Not only did he have to let go of the niggling details, he had to take the first steps toward reserving for himself the role that only the CEO/founder can play, that of leader and visionary. He needed a managerial structure in place to let him focus on his real job of growing the company.

Systems and Structures

When the management structure is in place, systems are never far behind. There's a reason why: both systems and structure are logical responses to complexity, which grows almost exponentially as the company expands. Shannan Marty had that experience. She is CEO of Tracer Research Group, a $15 million, Tucson-based tank and pipeline leak-detection company that she co-founded as a two-person operation in 1983. "By about $8 million or 50 employees, it just gets too big to keep it all in your head any more, says Marty. "We knew we had to keep better track of things, so we created positions and brought in people to do that."

Many of the senior management hires came from much larger companies like Fina, US West, and Ramada. "They were all incredibly talented people," says Marty. "The company would not have been able to grow to where we are today without them." What they brought with them were the systems that her existing employees, who'd grown up with the company, didn't have—things like salary schedules, performance evaluations, information systems, and strategic-planning processes. However, bringing in outsiders can be tricky.

"In hindsight, I probably over-hired. Eventually a culture clash developed from the regimented hierarchical communication structures they were used to at their mega-corporations. It was strangling us. Our long-term technical employees were very unhappy and turnover was up."

In addition, Marty says, "I deferred a lot of decisions to this team and listened to their ideas and accepted them, even when it didn't feel right in my gut, because they were the 'experienced' ones. In reality, they were no more experienced then I was in an entrepreneurial company." Through mutual agreement and fairly generous severance packages, Marty eventually replaced the outside hires with the people who were number two behind them, many of whom were the ones originally in those positions.

Marty says in the future there will have to be more executive-level hires. "We will need their experience and expertise, again, to help us grow and to grow our internal team." However, next time she plans to hire those with experience in a company with 500–1,000 employees, not the mega-corporations like before, and "to keep the informality, open door atmosphere and group problem-solving energy we've historically had."

Data Drives Prediction

The ultimate goal of imposing structure and instituting systems is, of course, predictability. Unless a company has the ability to determine where it is today and project where it's going to be this week, this month, this quarter, and this year, it's not on a trajectory for growth. It might not even be on track for survival.

At McKinney Lumber in Muscle Shoals, AL, Joe McKinney built to nearly $50 million the small family business he inherited. Much of the company's success is owed to McKinney's almost slavish devotion to metrics and measurements. McKinney started by training his entire workforce to understand terms like "gross margin" and "cost of sales" through having them operate a lunchtime sandwich business. He also established and popularized an internally understood Critical Number—a proprietary measurement of plant productivity he borrowed from another industry and modified to fit McKinney Lumber's business. The Critical Number tells the entire corporation, day to day, whether there's profit headed for the bottom line. "The idea of always measuring and tracking a Critical Number gives you a firm foundation to know where you are—even if you don't like the answer," chuckles McKinney.

It's the timeliness of the information that really sells the Critical Number concept for Mostly Muffins' Bolanos. "Two years ago, before we began tracking our progress daily, we had monthly statements from an accounting firm. It would be the third week in February before we knew how we did in January. Now, if we blow it in production or sales one day, we know it the next—and we're working with that team immediately to get them what they need."

Like everything else associated with growth, tracking for predictability becomes ever more difficult as revenues increase and the stakes become greater. "When we were measuring for a cake, a measuring cup worked fine," McKinney says. "But we needed a bigger bowl for a state dinner, and the accuracy had to be there—because a 2 percent error rate on 10 is nothing, but on 1,000, it's a miss by 20. So the tolerances of the system have had to tighten up as the company grows."

Top 5 Priorities

As you grow, you must keep the company focused. That's especially hard once you reach the point—usually at about 30 employees—where you can't personally interact with everyone each day. How do you keep everyone aligned and reading off the same page? Many gazelles find it useful to set priorities for each quarter—no more than five—and then to identify one goal that supersedes the others. This is known as a Top 5 and Top-1-of-5 priority list.

At Carney Interactive—a Virginia-based learning-solutions company that has gone from $1.9 million to $4.3 million in the past year and hopes to double again this year—founder and CEO John Carney keeps the Top 5 corporate priorities for the quarter and the company's eight core values on 8.5x11 laminated sheets posted inches from his employees' noses. Also on the sheet is a place for each employee to write his or her own Top 5 priorities for the quarter, aligning them with the company's Top 5. These postings remind the workforce what's important—like the priority this quarter to bring projects in on budget (they had started to miss a few) and core values like the need to adapt to rapid change and wisely manage corporate resources. These postings also serve as a simple but effective quarterly performance-appraisal system.

But Carney also likes the impression the sheets leave with visitors. "When you walk somebody around the office and everybody has this four-color Top 5 and Top 1 of 5 hanging over their desks, you typically get, 'Wow.'" says Carney. "It sends a clear indication to a client, a banker, or a prospective employee that there's something different about how we do business. It gives them another level of comfort that we're staying focused and doing the right things."

Like many gazelles, Carney's company drives quarterly priorities with a theme. Choosing a space motif, Carney first set a "Launch" theme and introduced it at an all-company event held at The Challenger Center for Space Science Education. "Our current theme is 'Escape Velocity,' because as the organization is growing, we're escaping the old bonds of how we used to do business. It's like a spaceship escaping gravity—you've got to exert a lot of energy to do it." Each time the 40-member workforce hits a sales goal, there's a theme-related celebration, with prizes and recognition.

While many companies tend to focus their themes on sales goals, it's important to focus on other areas of the company as well. "We tend to pick a non-sales goal in our fourth quarter each year," says The Scooter Store's Harrison. The practice started when he began to notice that the sales engine was going full-tilt, but elsewhere in the operation, "the wheels were falling off." So Harrison established a futuristic "sy-fi" (systems-finance) theme that identified several critical areas for improvement—including a call for zero errors and defects, "which was, at that time, ridiculous." But it was achieved using a systematic process of tracking errors, gathering data as to why they were happening, and then using standard quality-improvement methods for getting to the root cause and solving the problem.

The following year, Harrison defined a "Customer WOW" theme that aimed to have customers saying "wow" whenever they interacted with the company. Harrison himself created the first wow, by riding an elephant into the employee kickoff meeting. Harrison set another demanding task in front of the group, one worthy of a wow if achieved. The goal was to cut back the time it takes to get a disabled customer's malfunctioning wheels fixed. "The industry average is seven days, but that's seven whole days that these people are immobile," Harrison says. "We got it down to a day."

Hokey as they may sound, quarterly themes are powerful goal motivators. They focus the entire workforce on that single, overriding quarterly target in a way that people can not only understand, but get excited about. Says Bolanos of Mostly Muffins, "It's amazing what you can accomplish when you get a hundred people all working on just 1 priority, instead of 27."

Meeting Rhythm

Themes create the focus and the fun, but what makes a quarterly goal achievable is a daily and weekly rhythm aimed at keeping everyone informed, aligned, and accountable. One of the most successful practices any would-be gazelle can implement is that of a daily huddle—no more than 15 minutes per group, in a room or on a daily conference call, just to celebrate progress toward goals or identify barriers blocking that progress. Rockefeller had such a meeting rhythm with his executives every day of the 19 years he spent building Standard Oil. He was also a fanatic for metrics and priorities. These three Rockefeller Habits—priorities, data, and rhythm—are the key tools for handling the barriers that come with growth and keeping the company aligned. (See Chapter 2, Mastering the Right People Doing the Right Things Right, for more details about the three Rockefeller Habits.)

"In just 45 minutes from 9 to 9:45 every morning, we align the entire company," says Molly Bolanos of Mostly Muffins. "First it's the executive team, then the departments. You stick to your Top 5 [goals] and your Top 1 of 5, you identify your roadblocks, report your numbers and then, bye." These daily meetings serve to keep people informed, of course, but they also serve to put out fires that would otherwise clutter up the agenda of the weekly meeting, where the main topic must be the quarterly goals.

This rhythmic pulsing of daily and weekly meetings constitutes the real heartbeat of a growing company. To make the best possible use of these sessions, some companies set aside a special huddle area, where the walls are mapped with the top priorities, core values, metric charts, and market data. "Our executive team calls ours the Situation Room, because we're surrounded by the stuff that's big-picture important to us," says Doug Harrison of the Scooter Store. "It works. The fact that we meet there keeps us focused."

Maybe it seems too mind-blowing to even consider slowing down enough to institute a daily and weekly meeting structure, but gazelles that have done it are thrilled with the result. "I had heard about 'stand-up meetings' for years and had even tried it," says Alan Rudy of Express-Med. "It just became a test of endurance to stand for 30 minutes or more. We often finished just because we were tired, not because the business was getting done." Today the company's meetings typically run 10 minutes or less following a routine of just reporting the numbers, going around and highlighting bottlenecks or goal achievements, and being diligent about taking it off-line if a couple of people get involved in problem solving.

"It's true what they say: Routine sets you free. I don't love structure. It's just what I have to do, [if] I want to do all the things that I want to do," says Rudy. "And a pulse of 200 beats a year from 300 hearts in the company, now, that's a lot of blood flowing in the right direction."

Market Dynamics

The market can make you look smart or dumb, as we've all seen this past few years. Move with a trend and you win; try and buck a market movement and it can crush you. For architect Steve Smith of The Lawrence Group Companies in St. Louis, that point came about six years into his practice. Specializing in designing and building radio stations (the company also focuses in the healthcare and university arenas), Smith started witnessing the consolidation of the radio industry and felt he needed to respond in sync with the market. Yet he was going to have to think differently than his competitors, who view being an architect as a profession, not a business. "Most architects think about designing a building. We decided that we're about designing a business, and then finding people that design the buildings—which, in our case, is mostly radio station buildings."

This change of mindset, combined with the rise of the Internet, another market force he's embraced, has allowed Smith to create a business model that calls for a centrally managed network of architectural practices nationwide. So far, The Lawrence Group has expanded to five different cities, growing from 20 to 125 people and $1.5 million to $16 million in revenue since 1996. Smith firmly believes that 20 or 30 locations are possible. This growth-oriented mode of thinking "is a differentiator for us in our profession," says Smith, "while bringing us the same challenges everyone faces with growth." Smith went further than thinking big. He conceived a set of core values in his business (see

Chapter 4, Mastering the Use of Core Values) and put in the systems, metrics, and structures necessary to deal with the complexity. He's built the culture and discipline that, in 2000, got The Lawrence Group voted "the best place to work" in St. Louis for his size category of firms.

With growth, market pressures increase and strategic decisions come with higher stakes. At $10 million and higher, CEOs often feel their attention is being pulled inside the business just when they most need to be focusing on what's happening outside in the market. McKinney of McKinney Lumber says that hard experience has taught him that growth decisions are dangerous if you don't have a good feel for what's going on both inside and outside the business.

"You have to understand where you are within your own industry and know that you've got everything handled before you try to step up to the next level, because a fall off the side of that mountain can be deadly," McKinney says. "There are points along the way when you've got to get across the entire canyon to the next growth plateau in one jump. You don't get two jumps. But maybe you don't have to jump at all. Maybe the tigers on this side aren't as mean as the lions on the other side."

The plain truth is that growing a gazelle can be so painful at certain stages that many an otherwise successful CEO has looked to an exit strategy. Shannan Marty was sufficiently distressed with Tracer Research Group's flagging fortunes just last year that she was ready to sell—until a technological breakthrough captured the markets attention and convinced her and her partner to abandon the sale. Back in 1999, when Express-Med was struggling, Alan Rudy was considering either quitting or scaling back the business to a point where it might seem fun again.

Grow Thyself

But tough times offer good CEOs the opportunity to look at themselves and their role with new eyes. Molly Bolanos of Mostly Muffins says increased managerial sophistication through executive training and coaching has allowed her to re-evaluate and re-define her role. "I've realized that my unique ability is connecting with people—selling who we are and where we're going. I don't have to manage the numbers anymore, because I have a structure doing that for me. The potential now seems endless. Now, when I think about how to grow the company, the key strategic question is, 'Who do I need to be, and what do I have to do to get there?'"

With consulting help, Rudy realized he had been giving his middle managers too little authority and too many confusing instructions. He backed off, took some training to work on his personal style, and gave many of his day-to-day oversight functions to a newly hired president. Thanks to the management structures he's put in place, along with the measurements and meetings that keep it all humming, Rudy is free to work on new projects and acquisitions.

"It's absolutely amazing how all of this has changed our company," he says. "Today I have time to think and try things. This is my true talent—listening to what people need, talking to competitors and customers, and adjusting my business accordingly. When I am focusing solely inside the company, I cannot move the company ahead. I am much more the CEO than I was before."

Today, Rudy is back on an annual growth path of more than 50 percent, creating the kind of gazelle that is fun, and generating returns for himself and the economy—which add to the rewards of growing a business. This, too, is within your reach if you choose to make the leap.

Barriers to Growth

There are roughly 23 million firms in the US, of which only 4 percent get above $1 million in revenue. Of those firms, only about 1 out of 10, or 0.4 percent of *all* companies, ever make it to $10 million in revenue and only 17,000 companies surpass $50 million. Finishing out the list, the top 2,500 firms in the US are larger than $500 million and there are 500 firms in the world larger than $11 billion. As organizations move up this growth path they go through a predictable series of evolutions and revolutions *(Figure 1-1)*.

Let's review the three barriers that prevent firms from moving along this path: lack of leadership, lack of systems and structures, and market dynamics.

Leadership

As goes the leadership team goes the rest of the firm. Whatever strengths or weaknesses exist within the organization can be traced right back to the cohesion of the executive team and their levels of

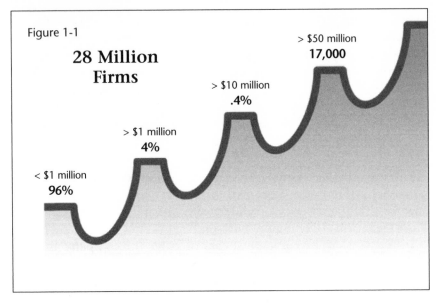

Figure 1-1

28 Million Firms

> $50 million
17,000

> $10 million
.4%

> $1 million
4%

< $1 million
96%

trust, competence, discipline, alignment, and respect. The two most important attributes of effective leaders are their abilities to predict and to delegate. Within the category of prediction I include the ability to set a compelling vision that anticipates market movements. Leaders don't have to be years ahead, just minutes ahead of the market, the competition, and those they lead. And the ability to accurately predict revenues and earnings is the ultimate test of leadership from the perspective of Wall Street and the public markets.

If we look at the second attribute of effective leadership, the ability to delegate, we can understand why most firms have fewer than ten employees. Getting others to do something as good as or better than yourself is one of the hardest aspects of leadership, but necessary if you're going to grow the business. Thus most entrepreneurs prefer to operate alone or with a couple of people. To get to the level of ten employees, the founders must at least begin to delegate those functions in which they are weak. As the organization approaches 50 employees, whatever is the strength of the top leader can become the weakness of the organization. From 50 employees up, it's then a matter of adding various layers of mid-level and frontline leaders. The success of the firm is determined by the extent to which the senior leadership team can grow the next levels of leadership, and teach them in turn to predict and delegate effectively.

Successful delegation starts with choosing the right person. Keep in mind the rule that one great person can replace three good people. With the right people, delegation is a four-step process to pinpoint what they are to do, create a measurement system for monitoring progress, provide feedback, and then give out appropriately timed recognition and reward.

Systems and Structures

As an organization grows it becomes more complex. There are mathematical formulas for complexity that show that as you move from two products, employees, or sites to four products, employees, or sites, your complexity increases by a factor of 12. It's a force of nature: the lowly amoeba can do everything it needs with one cell, but as the number of cells increase the organism begins to develop subsystems—for feeding, elimination, circulation, procreation, etc. The same is true for companies. Increases in complexity leads to stress, miscommunications, costly errors, poor customer service, and greater overall costs.

To keep from being buried, an organization must put in place appropriate systems and structures. When you go from two employees to ten, you need better phone systems and more structured space. If your company goes to 50 employees, you still need space and phones, but suddenly you need an accounting system that shows more precisely whether, which, and how projects, customers, or products are actually making money. From 50 employees (or from $10 to $50 million in revenue), typically all the information-technology systems need to be upgraded. And above $50 million, you get to revamp them again, as the organization tries to tie all systems to one database of customers and employees.

Considering structures, as the firm grows it becomes increasingly important to pay attention to organizational-structure issues. The key is to think in terms of three types of organizational charts. The first looks like what most of us know as the standard hierarchical organizational chart. I call it an accountability chart. The second type is actually a set of organizational charts that map work process or work flow. The third, the Almost Matrix, maps the relationships between organizational functions and the various business units that begin to form as the organization grows.

Accountability charts: A company will often become stuck or experience a lot of miscommunications and balls getting dropped when there isn't clear accountability established within an organization. All projects, line items on an income statement, priorities, and processes must ultimately be owned by a single person, even though there might be hundreds of people who have some kind of sub-accountabilities and responsibilities in seeing something completed.

There are two basic rules accompanying the creation of an accountability chart. First, there can be no "to be determined's" on the chart. If you can conceive of a position, put someone's name in it, even if his or her only accountability is to make sure the position is filled. Organizations often place the term "acting" in front of the title of someone filling a spot until it can be permanently filled.

Second, there are always a few people in the organization who shouldn't be leading other people, yet are considered senior in the organization. In this case, a few "off org chart" positions are advisable.

Work process charts: Because the accountability chart can't capture all the interactions necessary to run a business without a mass of dotted lines running all over the chart, it's better to keep the accountability chart clean and then establish four to nine work flow charts representing the critical processes that flow through the organization. These processes might include how you acquire a customer, how a project moves through the organization, how employees are selected and trained, and how customers are billed and payments collected. It's advisable to take the one process per quarter that seems the most dysfunctional and clean it up. Processes are like garages and hallway closets, which become messed up over time and require regular attention.

Almost Matrix: This chart shows the relationships between organizational functions and the business units that form as the organization grows. These units begin to feel and act like separate businesses within the business. They can be organized around product lines, customer niches, geographical locations, or business units acting as wholly owned subsidiaries of the parent company. Conflicts often arise between the functional leaders, like the VP of Sales and Marketing, and the business unit heads who have sales people driving their revenue. The key question is, to whom do the sales people report in the organization? This kind of tension often leads to a regular cycle of centralizing and then de-centralizing certain functions within the organization, which can consume a lot of energy. Our position is that most people should be accountable to the business unit leaders; the role of the functional leader is one of coaching and bringing best practices into the organization. It's a complex issue that requires some real thought and expertise.

Overall, it's important to think in terms of multiple organizational charts and to assign accountability to someone to make sure the various charts are being updated.

Market Dynamics

The market makes you look either smart or dumb. When it's going your way, it covers up a lot of mistakes. When fortunes reverse, all your weaknesses seem to be exposed. And there's a counter-intuitive aspect of growing a business: when the firm is under $10 million in revenue and just a little more focus internally on establishing healthy organizational habits would pay off in the long run, you have a tendency to focus mostly externally. In turn, as the organization passes $10 million, the organizational complexity issues start drawing the attention of the senior team inward at a time when it's probably more important for the team to be focused more on the marketplace. This is when it's useful to have outside assistance in dealing with internal issues so you can remain focused externally.

Going back to the evolution and revolution chart and considering the basic measures of a business—revenue, gross margin, profit, and cash—there is an important sequence of things to focus on. Between start-up and the first million or two in revenue, the key driver is revenue. The focus is on getting interest in the marketplace interested in you.

As for cash, the entrepreneur has to rely on self-funding or friends and family in the very beginning.

Between $1 million and $10 million, you add to your focus on revenue the cash concerns you had been putting off. Since the organization will typically grow more and faster during this stage than any other, cash will be rapidly consumed. In addition, in this stage the organization is experimenting a great deal to figure out what its specific focus and position in the market should be. These experiments can be costly.

As the organization passes $10 million, internal and external pressures come to the forefront. Externally, the organization is now on more radar screens, alerting competitors to your threats. Customers are beginning to demand lower prices as they do more business with your organization. At the same time, internal complexities increase, which cause costs to rise faster than revenue. All of this begins to squeeze an organization's gross margin. As gross margin slips a few points the organization is starved of the extra money it needs to invest in infrastructure like accounting systems and training, creating a snowball effect as the organization passes the $25-million mark. It's now critical that the company maintains a clear value proposition in the market to prevent price erosion. At the same time the company must continually simplify and automate internal processes to reduce costs. Organizations successful at doing both can actually see their gross margins increase during this stage of growth.

By $50 million in revenue an organization is expected to have enough experience and position in the marketplace that it can accurately predict profitability. Not that profit hasn't been important all along as the organization grows. It's just more critical at this stage that an organization can *predict* profitability, since a few point swings either way represents millions of dollars. This brings us full circle to the number one function of a leader, the ability to predict. The fundamental journey of a growing business is to create a *predictable* engine for generating wealth as it creates products and services that satisfy customer needs and creates an environment that attracts top talent.

In summary, growing a business is a dynamic process that requires a shifting set of priorities as the leadership team navigates the predictable evolutions and revolutions of growth. Continuing to grow the capabilities of leadership throughout the organization; installing systems and structures to manage increasing complexities; and moving ahead with the market dynamics that impact the business, are fundamental to successfully growing a business that's fun and profitable.

2

MASTERING THE RIGHT PEOPLE DOING THE RIGHT THINGS RIGHT

Optimize Your Human Capital!

Executive Summary: This chapter provides an overall framework for what decisions need to be made to increase the value of your business. It aligns nicely with Jim Collins' new research in what it takes to make a good firm great. And it provides a framework for applying the three Rockefeller Habits, which will be covered in this chapter.

There are three basic decisions an executive team must make:
1. Do we have the Right People?
2. Are we doing the Right Things?
3. Are we doing those Things Right?

The Right People

For 2000 and 2001, *Fortune* magazine surprised the business world by choosing The Container Store as #1 of the "Best Companies to Work

For," beating out standards like Southwest Airlines, GE, Microsoft and SAS. A 25-store retail chain that sells products that help you organize your home, it was launched 24 years ago by Kip Tindell and Garrett Boone, who were still leading the firm at the time this book was written. If you go to their Website, www.containerstore.com, and click on Careers, you'll see their hiring philosophy. In essence, they firmly believe that one great person can replace three good people.

They also pay their people 50 to 100 percent more than typical retailers, which can be done if you have proportionately fewer people. They also provide them with over 200 hours of training their first year versus the ten hours standard in the retail industry. Not two to three times the amount of training, but over 20 times the amount of training. And, again, this isn't GE I'm talking about. This is a firm in the retail business where the majority of the employees are college students who aren't likely to make a career out of working there.

Obviously, a key to The Container Store's success is that they have the Right People. And their formula is fairly simple; fewer people, paid more and given lots of training and development. Worried about spending all that money on training people so they can go elsewhere? The research is definitive that training and development increases loyalty. Besides, what's the alternative? Do you really want the people you have right now to not be the best trained for the job they have to do?

The first question you must ask is "Do I have the Right People?" And a quick way to discern the answer is to ask yourself if you would enthusiastically rehire each person on your team if given the opportunity. The second question to ask, especially regarding your executive team and other key employees, is whether you think they have the potential to be the best in their position three to five years from now. (By the way, you might have the Right People, just in the wrong position.) When you have "A" players, it makes all the difference in the world.

Hiring—Selling the Vision

Books have been written exclusively on the subject of hiring. (I'll mention an important one later in this chapter). However, there are a few basics to hiring that can go a long way toward making sure you're getting the right people. The first is to understand that hiring is a numbers game. The firms that get the best people tend to get a lot of people applying for each position and the general quality of the pool of people is so high that if you had to decide by throwing a dart at a list of potential employees you likely would make a great decision. And this is why a firm that has established a stellar reputation in its industry (or even in a particular town if you primarily hire locally) is able to continue to hire stellar people.

So ask yourself the question: did we get a lot of high-quality people to apply for the last position we hired, especially if it was an executive position? This applies whether you used a headhunting firm (do they have access to a large pool of quality applicants?) or you're driving the process yourself. Generally speaking, you or your headhunter should have an initial pool of 50 high-quality people to choose from. If you're relying on your network of contacts to find someone, are you reasonably sure they are in contact with a large pool of high-quality people? Remember, "A" people tend to surround themselves with "A" people, so go only to your "A" network of friends. I'm very serious about this last comment.

A useful tool you can use to access a high-quality pool of applicants, or any source of people—for example, for funding or getting a referral to a top executive at a potential customer—is to make a simple Top 10 list. I've done this with many CEOs looking to fill key positions. Take out a piece of paper and write down at least 10 people (20 is best) you could e-mail tomorrow who have contact with the kinds of people you want. Then put together a two-paragraph summary describing your firm, the position, and the kind of person you want to hire. Make it a point to call the people on your list as quickly as possible and let them know you're sending the summary by e-mail. Follow-up a week later to see if they know anyone or if they at least know someone who might know someone. This, by the way, is essentially what headhunters do, so if you're unwilling to do this, hire a headhunter.

Another important basic for hiring, whether you're sending out an e-mail, placing ads, using a headhunter, or utilizing several of the online services like monster.com, is to make sure you're truly selling the company and its vision. You need to market your firm to potential employees with the same vigor you use to attract potential customers. As shown in the following example, I had a client that simply changed their ad from the first one to the second one and increased the number of applicants three-fold:

EMPLOYMENT AD—Exceptional opportunity! Rapidly growing promotional marketing agency with Fortune 500 clients seeking: ACCOUNT EXECUTIVE (description only delineating qualifications).

versus

WHEN WAS THE LAST TIME YOU HAD FUN AT WORK? It's a great time to join our promotional marketing agency team. Get all the benefits of working with Fortune 500 clients in a small-agency environment. Not only do we take pride in what we do, we have FUN. Your creativity & energy are what we need. PROMOTIONS MANAGER description (delineating what you'll do) and ACCOUNT EXECUTIVE description. Enjoy coming to work. Send resume to_____.

If using a headhunter, work with them to create a persuasive description of the company and position they can share.

The Selection Process

Interviewing is the most perilous part of the process because there is actually a slight negative correlation between who you would likely hire based on an interview and whether they would be a great fit with your firm. Given how badly many people conduct interviews, you would be better off throwing darts at a list! The only type of interview that is effective is a behavior-based structured interview. Bradford Smart is *the* expert in this field. I highly recommend his latest book *Topgrading.* It's very "how-to."

Testing is considerably more accurate and objective than interviewing and should always supplement the interview process. Many of the best-run firms have their applicants, especially potential executives or managers, submit to several hours of formal testing. Least important of the tests, though the one everyone seems to use, is the standard personality test. Don't mess around in this arena—use professionals to help with this process. My firm recommends to all clients Bartell & Bartell, (814-861-6606) for manager and executive hires. It will cost you roughly $600 per candidate, so we recommend doing the testing on the top three picks. And you'll need to have yourself tested so they can check for compatibility. For the rest of your hires we recommend Bigby Havis & Associates' online testing products (972-233-6055). Again, you need to have yourself tested.

I've interviewed candidates in the afternoon, had them go online in the evening and complete tests and had the results available immediately online so the decision can be made the next morning.

The most important thing you're trying to discern in the selection process is the candidate's fit with your culture. See Chapter 4, Mastering the Use of Core Values for more on this. If you've discovered your core values properly and they are alive in your organization, the number one reason an otherwise-qualified candidate just won't make it in your organization is his or her misalignment with your core values. A close second is whether they have a positive or negative outlook, which can be discerned primarily through testing. For entrepreneurial companies, a positive outlook is a requirement. Testing for emotional maturity also ranks high on my general recommendation list as an important "go, no go" factor in the hiring decision. Last, I recommend and use a variation of an assessment-center approach. Outline on a piece of paper three or four business challenges you're expecting candidates to face when hired and then give them 30 minutes to an hour to work through how they would handle each. Then spend another 30 minutes working through their solutions with them to see how they think and to get a sense how you might work together. If nothing else, when I've employed this technique I've picked up even from the candidates I've not hired some great insights into business challenges I'm facing. One time I even contracted with a candidate to do a special project, even though the candidate knew I wasn't offering a permanent position.

Though not always possible, the best way to select the Right Person is to have someone work with you for several weeks doing the work you're expecting him or her to do. For frontline hires, "temp-to-perm" placement firms are popular because they allow you to test-drive the candidate. For management hires, see if they can work with you in the evenings on a consulting basis. Several of my venture capital friends have found, especially when hiring a top executive, that nothing substitutes for simply working alongside the final candidate over an extended period of time dealing with the tough issues facing the business. That's why promoting from within and hiring people you've worked with in the past are so effective.

Overall, getting the right people in the right positions is *the* first and most important job of the CEO and executive team. Also important is getting the wrong people out as quickly as possible—though for many reasons this is one of the hardest aspects of running a business. It's why you need a strong executive team and a top-notch advisor so they can tell you when you're blind to the obvious facts. Often you just can't see the problem people yourself.

Right Things Model

The Right Things Right model *(Figure 2-1)* illustrates the fundamental decisions, relationships and functions of a business. The three ovals on the left side of the model show the Right Things; the three ovals on the right show how to do Things Right. Every business theory can be mapped onto the model; it provides a framework with which to integrate various business theories. It's also a useful model to help explain to all employees the fundamentals of business. Lastly, it serves as a useful tool for choosing quarterly priorities.

The key questions on the Right Things side of the model are "Do you have a viable economic model?" Or, more bluntly, can you ever make real money doing what you're doing? Do you have a product or service that enough customers value to make a viable business? And have you determined the X factor that you can control that differentiates you from the competition, matters to customers and provides you an advantage in the marketplace? Can you be the best in your chosen sandbox?

The key questions on the Things Right side of the model are "Do you have the management practices and processes to take advantage of the market opportunity you're pursuing?" Do you have the habits and disciplines in place to maintain your competitive advantage? Is your organization structured properly to maximize the productivity of the employees? Can you deliver a consistent service or product offering?

Moving down through the model, you know you're doing the Right Things when revenue or market share—or both—are growing at twice the market. Though most executives feel their business is unique, you can always approximate the growth of your industry segment from various sources. And if your industry segment is in decline, are you growing at least twice as fast as your nearest competitor as you divide up what's left as others exit the market? You know you're doing Things Right when your gross margins and profitability are at the top of your industry. Again, you can approximate these numbers.

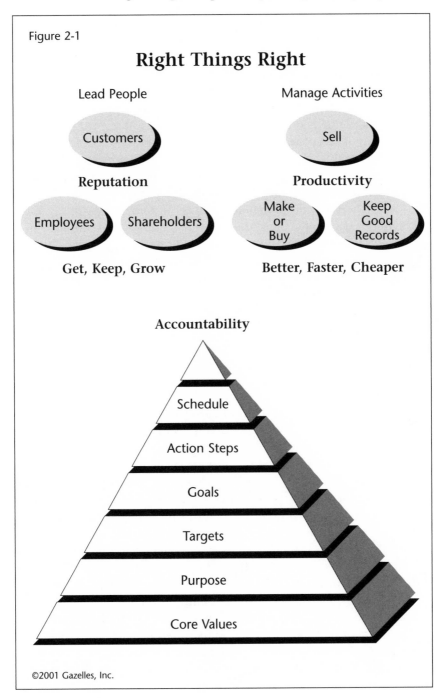

Figure 2-1

Right Things Right

Lead People

Customers

Reputation

Employees   Shareholders

Get, Keep, Grow

Manage Activities

Sell

Productivity

Make or Buy   Keep Good Records

Better, Faster, Cheaper

Accountability

Schedule

Action Steps

Goals

Targets

Purpose

Core Values

©2001 Gazelles, Inc.

The Right Things side requires bold leadership able to make a few key decisions about strategy and direction, especially when the business needs to make an abrupt turn in the market—like Microsoft's decision to shift significant resources to the Internet or Bill Gates' decision to step down as CEO. The Things Right side requires capable management that can maintain healthy disciplines and habits. Interestingly, much of what is good management is being augmented by and will eventually be replaced by technology so that the people in the organization can focus more on leading instead of managing. Our firm has created some executive management automation systems that are already heading down this path.

If you then consider that a business is simply "people" doing "activities," the model supports a familiar notion that you lead people and manage their activities—you don't manage people. Think of the parenting approach that says you love the child while being tough on their inappropriate behaviors, i.e. "son, you're good, what you did is bad" versus "son, you're bad." It's important to separate the person from their activities. While continuing to inspire people through your leadership skills, you must also be diligent about holding people accountable to results. In fact, you might have to love someone enough to let him or her go. (I tend to prefer the phrase "freeing up your future!")

This is where the model gets more explicit. The Right Things side represents the people and relationships involved in any business; the Things Right side represents the activities or transactions that occur within a business to deliver consistent products and services to the market. The three fundamental groups of people that interact in a business are Customers (including suppliers), Employees (including sub-contractors), and Shareholders—which models closely the Balanced Scorecard system UPS and other firms have adopted. (There's a book called *The Balanced Scorecard* for those interested—it essentially supports the notion that a leader's success is defined as having satisfied all three stakeholders, not just one or two.) The three fundamental activities at the heart of all businesses are the functions of Making or Buying something, Selling something, and Keeping Good Records. This mirrors the primary top executive functions of COO (make or buy), VP Sales and Marketing (sell), and CFO (records), with the CEO serving as their leader. Though the titles may vary, it's this fundamental troika serving under the CEO that makes an effective organization.

Taking the model further, on the Right Things side you strive to achieve three outcomes: get, keep and grow all three relationships. To do this, you need to figure out what basic needs you can fill for a certain group of customers in a way that differentiates you from the competition and then what competencies your people need to meet those needs so that value is created for the shareholders. I was specific in using the term "needs" versus "wants." Customers can bankrupt you with their wants, wants, wants while a laser-focused competitor can come along and deliver on a more important need and steal your customers. Ultimately, this boils down to one overarching concept—the fundamental need to build a great reputation with all three stakeholders. You know you have a great reputation when it gets easier, instead of harder, to get, keep, and grow each of the three relationships

On the Things Right side, the organization strives to achieve three additional outcomes: doing each of the activities better, faster, and cheaper. The primary objective is to continue to lower the costs of delivering your products or services relative to the sales price and improve the value proposition so you can maintain your prices relative to the competition to increase profitability. The right side of the model encapsulates the classic, "buy low, sell high, and keep good records" fundamentals of business.

Looking at the Right Things Right model from a pure accounting perspective, the left side of the model represents the balance sheet of the business, delineating who owes and who owns what. The bottom line of a balance sheet is net worth—a measure of value created for the shareholders. The right side of the model represents the income statement (P&L), delineating the revenues and expenses with a bottom line of profitability.

The six circles of the Right Things Right model balance on the vision of the company, as represented by the Planning Pyramid shown at the bottom of Figure 2-1. This will be covered in Chapter 3, Mastering a One-Page Strategic Plan. It's the vision of the company, from its core values to its specific accountabilities, that gives a focus to the specifics of each of the six circles—exactly who are the customers, employees, and shareholders, and exactly what are the activities in which the business will engage. What's important to note at this point is that there is a constant balancing act between the left and right sides of the model; between driving revenue and making sure the business is profitable; between having enough people and having enough activities for those people; between protecting the reputation of the firm and increasing the productivity of the firm. Business is a constant process of balancing priorities, which is why the top part of the model balances on the pinpoint vision of the company.

Putting the Model to Work

In addition to a general framework for business, there are three specific uses of the model relative to the Rockefeller Habits:

Rockefeller Habit # 1—Priorities

A starting point to figuring out the number one priority for any particular quarter is to consider the six circles as potential priorities and choose the one on each side that needs the most attention at that moment. Be sure to specify whether the left-side driver is get, keep, or grow, and whether the right-side driver is better, faster, or cheaper. As an example, this quarter the top priority might be "increase by 25 percent (grow) the business we're doing with our top four customers" (choosing the Customers circle on the left) and "reduce the time by 50 percent (faster) it takes to properly bill our clients" (choosing the Keep Good Records circle on the right). Even though your firm may have issues within all six areas, you can only advance one of the areas on each side at a time. And because they are all interconnected, by giving momentum to one you provide momentum to all. Selecting a specific area is one of the tougher disciplines to maintain because the tendency is to try and work on all the areas simultaneously. However, leaders find that when they focus everyone's energies around one area, it gets fixed much more quickly. Two visual analogies are helpful. First, think of the six circles as spinning plates on sticks, like you might have seen on an old Ed Sullivan rerun. At any one time, one of the plates of the three on either side is spinning slower than the other two and needs your attention. Another way to think of the six circles is as balls being juggled in the air. As a juggler moves the balls higher and higher, he or she does it one ball at a time. The same situation applies to growing a business. It's a process of hiring employees, rounding up customers, then making sure you have cash to support the growth, as you hire more employees.... The process is never-ending.

In addition, it's very important to be clear about who is accountable for each circle in the model. Who is accountable for getting customers? Who is accountable for keeping shareholders happy? Who is accountable for making sure the sales engine (the Sell circle) is functioning properly? Going through each of the six circles and their drivers (get, keep, grow, and better, faster, cheaper) and making sure the accountabilities are clear is one of the more powerful and aligning activities I've worked on with executive teams.

Rockefeller Habit #2—Data

To monitor the progress of the business daily and weekly, and to accurately predict how the next few months are likely to turn out, you need metrics about all six areas of the business. For mid-market firms, the weakness on the left side of the model is having the same kind of accurate and timely feedback from customers that you demand from accounting. On the right side of the model, mid-market firms tend to be weak in having accurate sales funnel data, primarily because the sales side of the organization tends to resist measurement, except for the top line.

Rockefeller Habit #3—Rhythm

In figuring out with whom you need to have various weekly meetings, the six circles provide guidance. On the right side of the model, it's crucial that operations, sales, and accounting each has its own daily and weekly rhythms. In turn, it's important that the executive team have some rhythm in terms of meeting with customers and employees. And if you are a public company, you have an entire new set of rhythms that revolve around the shareholder circle.

Organizational Structure

Besides giving substance to the Rockefeller Habits, the six circles provide guidance for the changing organizational structure necessary to handle growth. Around $10-million in revenue, the three fundamental functions represented by the three circles on the right begin to split. The Sell circle splits into separate sales and marketing functions, requiring different personalities to head up each. (As a side note, the key measurable for marketing or business development is lead generation.) The Make or Buy circle splits into separate operations and R&D functions (or their equivalents—all firms should have some form of R&D). And the Keep Good Records circle splits into separate accounting and finance departments. On the left side of the model, growing firms tend to develop more specific functional areas focusing on employees, (HR is the old term); focusing on customers, whereby the organization starts to create customer-focused teams to complement possible product-focused teams; and focusing on shareholders where public firms develop specific shareholder-relations departments.

In summary, the Right People Doing the Right Things Right model encompasses the fundamental decisions leaders must make to successfully drive any business. The rest of the book provides specific tools for addressing each of these areas.

3

MASTERING A ONE-PAGE STRATEGIC PLAN

Keeping it simple keeps it clear!

Executive summary: The bigger your company gets, and the faster it's growing, the harder it is to get everybody on the same page. The problem, of course, is that there isn't a single page around which to align. Instead, there are likely more than a dozen pages, actual and imaginary, along with memos and e-mails, each purporting to describe your company's vision, mission, and strategy. Further, many of these messages may be riddled with unclear and even contradictory statements about who your company is, what it does, and how. This chapter will introduce you to the Planning Pyramid and the One-Page Strategic Plan, a simple yet powerful tool that helps you edit your vision and strategy down to a single, action-oriented page. Go to www.gazelles.com to download for free an English, Spanish, or French editable Word version of the One-Page Strategic Plan and a more comprehensive document called "One-Page Strategic Plan: How to Complete."

Back when your company was just getting started, and you were struggling to get the job done with three or four key people, confusion over the vision was unheard of. Everybody was eating and sleeping the company's goals, just as you were. Your employees knew

29

as well as you did which task was critical because they all were! Rarely did people complain about communication problems.

But with each new level of growth, and each new hire, your influence over the organization necessarily grows more arm's-length. You begin to delegate low-level strategic decisions, and not surprisingly, some of the calls your associates make leave you scratching your head. Perhaps misunderstandings have cropped up between associates, each side believing they were doing what they were supposed to. Maybe customers are complaining about mistakes, or—worse—neglect. The ugly truth is plain: the vision and strategy that always seemed so clear to you, as the entrepreneurial brains of the company, have gotten muddled somewhere along the way. Where once you could relay an idea to a handful of close associates and have it understood and implemented immediately, you now find it takes days or weeks to get the concept out laterally. Then it might take more weeks, even months, to communicate the information to the lowest levels of the organization. And when you're done, people will still clamor for more and better communication.

If you're thinking, "Yes, but that's just how it is when companies get bigger," you should know that there are tools for handling the increasing complexity business growth generates. Maybe there was a time when companies could rationalize their poor internal communication as just the unfortunate by-product of success. Maybe they could get by from year to year, just resting on the laurels of a respected name and a commanding market share. If so, those days are long gone. Thanks to global competition, the rise of e-commerce and the ever-quickening pace of innovation, clear communication of an effective strategy is absolutely essential to survival. To become and remain competitive, your organization needs three things:

1. a **framework** that identifies and supports your corporate strategy,
2. a common **language** in which to express that strategy, and,
3. a well-developed **habit** of using this framework and language to continually evaluate your strategic progress.

Most important, you've got to keep it simple. Who has time to read—let alone develop—packets and pamphlets of forgettable prose? You've got to boil your expression of strategic might down to one powerful, useable, post-able, and thoroughly unforgettable page.

Meet the strategic framework that works best for emerging companies. It's called the Planning Pyramid *(Figure 3-1)*. As a consultant to

Figure 3-1

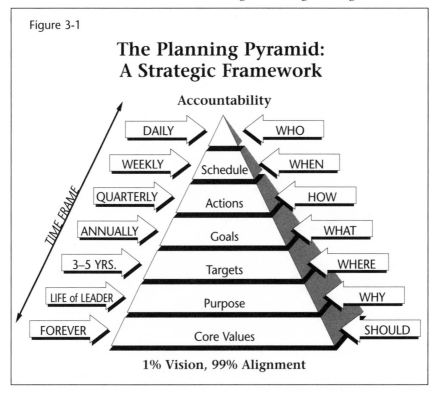

The Planning Pyramid:
A Strategic Framework

Accountability

DAILY — WHO

WEEKLY — Schedule — WHEN

QUARTERLY — Actions — HOW

ANNUALLY — Goals — WHAT

3–5 YRS. — Targets — WHERE

LIFE of LEADER — Purpose — WHY

FOREVER — Core Values — SHOULD

TIME FRAME

1% Vision, 99% Alignment

growing companies of all stripes and types for more than 20 years, I've seen what works in establishing an effective vision and I have incorporated these best practices into a concise tool. The pyramid graphically conveys to everyone in your organization how the various vision pieces—values, purpose, targets, goals, actions, schedules and accountabilities—align, establishing a common strategic language that is easy to use and helps eliminate confusion. The One-Page Strategic Plan *(Figure 3-2)* provides the tool for getting it all down on paper. A sample completed plan *(Figure 3-3)* can be found at the end of this chapter.

From the gazelles.com Website you may download an editable Word document; print it out and fill it in by hand. When you print it out, place the 1st page to the left of the 2nd page, giving you a continuous, single-page document on an 11-by-17-inch piece of paper.

If you don't want to do this right now, read through the rest of this chapter to give you a sense of the language and process I suggest for defining a whole vision. A vision is a dream with a plan. Without all

Figure 3-2

One-Page Strategic Plan

Organization Name: _____

Your Name: _____

Date: _____

Core Values/Beliefs (Should/Shouldn't)	Purpose (Why)	Targets (3-5 yrs.) (Where)	Goals (1 yr.) (What)
_____	_____	Future Date	Yr. Ending
_____	_____	Revenues	Revenues
_____	_____	Profit	Profit
_____	_____	Mkt Cap	Mkt Cap
_____	_____		Gross Margin
_____	_____	*Sandbox*	Cash
_____	_____		A/R Days
_____	_____		Inv. Days
_____	_____		Rev./Emp.
_____	*Actions* To Live Values, Purposes, BHAG	*Key Thrusts/ Capabilities* 3–5 Year Priorities	*Key Initiatives* Annual Priorities
_____	1	1	1
_____	2	2	2
_____	3	3	3
_____	4	4	4
_____	5	5	5
_____	Check boxes above after assigning accountability	Smart numbers	
_____	*BHAG*	*Brand Promise*	*1 or 2 Critical #s*
_____	_____	_____	_____
_____	_____	_____	_____
_____	_____	_____	_____
_____	_____	_____	_____

Figure 3-2 *(cont.)*

Opportunities to exceed plan		Threats to making plan	
1		1	
2		2	
3		3	
4		4	
5		5	

Actions (Qtr.) (How)		**Theme (Qtr./Annual)**	**Your Accountability** (Who/When)	
			Your Quarterly Priorities	Due
Qtr. #		Deadline	1	
Revenues		Measurable Target/ Critical #		
Profit			2	
Mkt Cap			3	
Gross Margin				
Cash		***Theme Name***	4	
A/R Days			5	
Inv. Days				
Rev./Emp.				

Rocks Quarterly Priorities		***Scoreboard Design*** Describe and/or sketch your design in this space.	
1			
2			
3			
4			
5			
Prioritize your Rocks			

1 or 2 Critical #s

Celebration/Reward

For editable Word document, go to www.gazelles.com

seven levels of the Planning Pyramid delineated, your vision will be less than complete.

The One-Page Strategic Plan is essentially the Planning Pyramid turned on its side. The tool aligns both horizontally and vertically, providing a logical framework for organizing your strategic vision and guaranteeing that you have all the pieces to make it whole. The physical structure of the tool forces prioritization, which is key.

No organization or individual can focus on or accomplish more than five or six priorities in a given time period. The One-Page Strategic Plan forces you to select what I call your Top 5 and Top 1 of 5 priorities. And as you fill in the document, think of it as a giant crossword puzzle, where figuratively speaking, seven across needs to align with three down—thus, if you can't immediately determine what should go in one box, like the BHAG, then figure out your Core Purpose and your Brand Promise, then triangulate into what your BHAG should be.

Filling in the One-Page Strategic Plan

Let's begin filling out the One-Page Strategic Plan (for a more extensive explanation which includes how to structure your strategic planning session go to www.gazelles.com and download the free document "One-Page Strategic Plan: How to Complete.") Place the name of the firm at the top of the left page. This isn't a trivial matter. I'm amazed how often there isn't alignment around the name of the firm, with some people using acronyms or shortened versions of the name. Or the firm may have recently undergone a name change. The Organization Name line is also useful in signifying whether the strategic vision applies to only a division or department within a firm, i.e. Gazelles' Accounting Department. Finish the title area by adding your own name and the date the document was filled out.

Opportunities and Threats

To the far upper right (top of the second page), you'll note space to fill in Opportunities and Threats. Many strategic planning sessions start with a SWOT analysis—Strengths, Weaknesses, Opportunities, and Threats. Use whatever method you like to conduct a SWOT analysis. From the planning organizer's perspective, the Strengths and

Weaknesses come to the surface as the body of the form is completed. As for the Opportunities and Threats, again, I apply the Top 5 rule. List the five biggest opportunities and threats facing the organization over whatever time period the planning session is considering—next quarter and the coming year if it's one of the quarterly review sessions, or the next three to five years if it's an annual planning session.

Core Values

Going to the body of the form and starting with the left column (which is also the base of the Planning Pyramid in its vertical form) write in the core values of the firm. These five to eight statements broadly define the *shoulds* and *shouldn'ts* that govern your company's underlying decisions. Think of them as the Ten Commandments or your constitution, the foundation upon which the rest of the vision is built. My firm, for instance, has six core values, which are listed on the sample One-Page Strategic Plan. For a more complete definition and process for discovering your core values, read Jim Collins' September–October, 1996 *Harvard Business Review* article entitled "Building Your Company's Vision" (go to www.hbr.com to download a copy for $6). I've chosen to align with our friend Jim's language. Jim was the co-author of *Built to Last,* which I consider to be one of the ten best business books ever written. (For help uncovering your core values, go to Chapter 4.)

Are you wondering if your firm might be too young or too small to have well-established core values? Such thinking is mistaken. All firms have an unwritten set of values right from the beginning, and you don't need to wait until you've reached 50 or 100 employees to commit them to writing. At Gazelles, we've known our core values and used them right from the start. They're especially valuable as a foundation for many of the people processes that are so essential to business.

Purpose

Once you've identified and internally ratified your core values, move up the One-Page Strategic Plan or to the next column of the plan, to Purpose. It answers the very basic why questions: Why is this company doing what it's doing? What's the higher purpose for why we're in the business we're in? Why do I have such passion for what we're doing?

The purpose gives the company heart. It also provides a clue as to why certain seemingly small incidents send the CEO into a tirade, while others that may be bigger and more costly in impact slide by almost without comment. For example, my purpose revolves around the word "freedom." A situation that challenges my freedom, such as unnecessary bureaucracy in my organization or somebody else's, absolutely brings up the hair on the back of my neck. Find what rankles the CEO in your firm, and you'll have a leg up on figuring out your company's purpose. My personal favorite purpose is Wal-Mart's "To give ordinary folks the chance to buy the same things as rich people."

Actions and BHAG

At the bottom of the Purpose column of the One-Page Strategic Plan you'll see the sections Actions and BHAG. Quarterly, you should take a look at your core values and your purpose statement. If your core values seem to be sagging, or your purpose isn't being fully realized, the action list affords you the opportunity to detail the specific actions the firm needs to take to bring things into better alignment. The BHAG is your Big Hairy Audacious Goal. As the name implies, it's a 10- to 25-year, lofty goal, similar to Kennedy's legendary goal to put a man on the moon. It's the sort of goal that challenges the firm to greatness. Again, look at Jim Collins' *Harvard Business Review* article for more detail on defining a purpose and a BHAG. You can also go to www.jimcollins.com and work through his free tutorials.

Targets and Sandbox

Next comes Targets. The Target level describes where you want the firm to be in 3 to 5 years. Besides listing certain quantifiable targets at the top of the column, a firm should define the Sandbox in which the company chooses to play, a place where it can be #1 or #2. The Sandbox defines the firm's expected geographical reach, product or service offering, and expected market share within the chosen three- to five-year time frame. And yes, your Sandbox can and often does change. Xerox changed its tag line to "The Document Company" to signify a change in Sandbox focus-from being a copier equipment seller to document management.

Brand Promise

Next, clearly articulate the key need you're going to satisfy for your customers—your measurable Brand Promise (often called a value-added proposition or differentiator). It's important that it be measurable, like FedEx's 10 a.m. delivery promise or Sprint's "pin drop" clarity. It's from this measurable promise that all other measures and processes derive. Chapter 9 will focus on this important subject of Brand Promise.

Key Thrusts/Capabilities

Now define five or six Key Thrusts/Capabilities necessary for you to dominate your defined Sandbox, fulfill your Brand Promise, and meet your quantifiable Targets. What are the five or six big things you need to do to reach your three- to five-year targets? Easier said than done, this part of the process challenges your team to define the handful of strategic moves that will put you on top.

Goals and Key Initiatives

We're halfway up the Pyramid and ready for the Goals level, the one that tackles the all-important issue of what your company needs to achieve in the coming year to realize your longer-term targets. Besides quantifying your goals for the year at the top of the column, list your five or six Key Initiatives for the year, similar in strategic importance to, and aligned with, the Key Thrusts/Capabilities. Think of these initiatives as your corporate New Year's resolutions, and plan to revise them each time you close the books on your fiscal year—or as the marketplace demands—while keeping an eye on the Targets column.

Critical Numbers

Another crucial part of the Goals level of the pyramid is the designation of one or two *Critical Numbers*—ideally, one from the balance sheet and one from the income statement. They should represent key weaknesses at the heart of your economic model or operations that, if addressed successfully, will have a significant and positive impact on the business. A Critical Number could be the utilization rates of service delivery personnel, or fundraising goals, or an increase in the number of large accounts to reduce corporate vulnerability. The key is to drive to a root cause and to change the Critical Numbers at least annually to focus energy on different parts of the organization. It's similar to rotating your workouts to focus on different muscle groups.

Actions and Rocks

Next come the quarterly action steps. This is the *how* stuff. Here's where you break down your annual goals into the quarterly action steps that lead to achieving your yearly goals. Think of them as a series of five or six simultaneous 13-week missions that provide priorities to your entire organization as you drive to achieve the quarterly missions. I label these quarterly missions Rocks to align with Stephen Covey's use of the term. Rocks are the priorities that need to stay out front, ahead of the fire fighting and pebble moving we do on a day-to-day basis. As was the case at the Goals level, you also need to figure out your Critical Numbers—this time, the quarterly Critical Numbers.

Theme, Scoreboard Design, and Celebration/Reward

Looking at your Rocks, Critical Numbers, and Goals for the year, establish a quarterly or annual Theme to bring additional focus to everyone's activities. Decide where to post a scoreboard that will keep everyone apprised of your progress toward achieving the measurable target of the theme. Don't forget the celebration either. You should state ahead of time what fun and exciting reward or event will occur when the measurable target is hit.

Looking Ahead

Now, before moving on to the next level of the pyramid, get out your corporate calendar and identify the dates of the next quarterly meeting. That's when you'll reconsider your theme and re-establish your action steps for a new quarter. Block in a full day for each of these quarterly sessions. Determining the appropriate action steps isn't as easy as it may sound. For most companies, they're the equivalent of running a mini-marathon. They take lots of preparation beforehand, and they burn up lots of time and managerial energy—that is, if you're doing them right. So, plan ahead!

Schedules

The second-to-last level of the Planning Pyramid is devoted to schedules and is represented in the last column of the One-Page Strategic Plan as a due date. Here's where the action steps from the previous level get elaborated into a more detailed chronology. Looking across the entire organization, you need to determine *when* things will happen. What happens first? What happens next? Which activities are linked cross-functionally, and what impact will these shared activities have on your ability to get things done? Take all of that into account when establishing your schedules. Start by having each executive who has accountability for a specific initiative or rock come back with a one-page outline of the steps—with dates—necessary to complete the tasks.

While struggling through the details involved in completing this part of the pyramid, remember: Nothing ever gets done in any organization until it shows up on somebody's weekly To Do list—and I do mean weekly! Quit thinking in monthly increments and drive all measurements, deadlines, and deliverables down to weekly increments. It may be painful in the doing, but it needs to be done.

Accountability

Last and most important, we cap our Planning Pyramid with some necessary accountability. This is the *who* level, where your company identifies specifically which person is accountable for which particular activity on your plan.

Please note that I didn't say you should identify who's "responsible," because responsibility and accountability are two quite different things. Many people are likely responsible for meeting a certain goal or creating a product, but there should never be more than one person who is accountable. It doesn't mean this person has to do

Figure 3-3

One-Page Strategic Plan

Organization Name: Gazelles, Inc.
Your Name:　　　 Verne Harnish
Date:　　　　　　December 20, 1999

Core Values/Beliefs (Should/Shouldn't)	Purpose (Why)	Targets (3-5 yrs.) (Where)	Goals (1 yr.) (What)
1 Ecstatic customers 2 Practice What We Preach 3 1st Class for Less 4 Honor Intellectual Capitalists 5 Everyone an Entrepreneur 6 Never, Ever Give Up	Freedom—Our actions create more, not less, freedom for our clients, associates, shareholders and the community.	Future Date 12/31/2004 Revenues $50 million Profit 15% Mkt Cap $100 million **Sandbox** 1000 "gazelle" clients with revenues between $5 million and $200 million	Yr. Ending 12/31/2000 Revenues $2.5 million Profit Breakeven Mkt Cap Gross Margin 40% Cash 400k A/R Days 45 Inv. Days Rev./Emp.
	Actions To Live Values, Purposes, BHAG 1 Hassles E-Mail 2 Master Agent Calls 3 Coach Feedback 4 Exploders 5 Check boxes above after assigning accountability	**Key Thrusts/ Capabilities** 3–5 Year Priorities 1 Gazelles.com with 15 million employees from 10,000 firms utilizing. 2 25 Master Agents fully functioning. 3 Major business publication partnership. 4 Community College initiative fully functional. 5 Creative exclusive image **Smart Numbers** Program Ratings Enrollment Numbers per Program Available Free Cash	**Key Initiatives** Annual Priorities 1 Gazelles.com funded and operating. 2 60 additional clients and 10 Master Agents. 3 Coach process nailed. 4 Implementation Kits for all content providers. 5 Test collecting 50% deposits to further improve positive cash flow. **1 or 2 Critical #s** 80 ecstatic customers giving us $4 million run rate.
	BHAG 10,000 clients as the #1 distribution channel of knowledge products and services to gazelles.	**Brand Promise** 100% implementation of ideas we teach. "Less knowledge and more action."	

Figure 3-3 *(cont.)*

Opportunities to exceed plan		Threats to making plan	
1	Gazelles.com	1	Not having a "whole solution"
2		2	Under capitalized clients
3		3	
4		4	
5		5	

Actions (Qtr.) (How)	Theme (Qtr/Annual)	Your Accountability (Who/When)
		Your Quarterly Priorities Date
Qtr. #1 Ending 3/31/2002	Deadline 2/29/00	1 Technology to Interliant
Revenues $400,000	Measurable Target/ Critical #	2 Coaches doing Juicers
Profit Breakeven	100% completion of 5 transactions	3 New Head Coach fully on board
Mkt Cap		
Gross Margin 40%		4 Implementation Kits for three content providers completed
Cash 250k	*Theme Name*	
A/R Days 60	Operation Transition	
Inv. Days		5 Test payment system with MBD6
Rev./Emp.		

Rocks Quarterly Priorities	**Scoreboard Design** *Describe and/or sketch your design in this space.*	
1 Gazelles.com prototype		
2 Head Coach/Coaching Process		
3 iGo Performance development process test		
4 Enough coaches to replace Verne doing one-day intro's (Juicer)		
5 Additional key content relationship		
Prioritize your rocks.		

1 or 2 Critical #s MBD5 full and happy and 2 additional Master Agents on board	**Celebration/Reward** $1000 bonus	
		For editable Word document, go to www.gazelles.com

everything or be the smartest or be the most senior. It simply means he or she is the one to give the activity a voice—to care that something is happening relative to the specific deliverable. Remember, if everyone's accountable then no one's accountable.

Doing the Right Things Right: Your Completed One-Page Strategic Plan

Congratulations, you've completed the One-Page Strategic Plan! Again, see my sample completed plan at the end of this chapter. One caution—resist the temptation to go back and revise or wordsmith your document. The point isn't finding the exact words, or using them perfectly. It's having something on a single sheet of paper that says it all for your company, no matter how imperfectly, and being able to use it daily to help your company reach its potential.

I've said it so often that I finally made it the headline above every One-Page Strategic Plan I distribute: You must remember that this process is 1 percent vision and 99 percent alignment. The lion's share of your effort must go not into meeting, talking, and wordsmithing, but toward getting your people aligned to do what needs to be done. Use your One-Page Strategic Plan daily, weekly, quarterly, and annually to "Do the right thing!"

4

MASTERING THE USE OF CORE VALUES

Use core values to parent a great company!

Executive summary: Having a few rules, repeating yourself a lot, and acting in ways that are consistent with the rules—these are the three keys whether you're providing your children with a good moral foundation or providing a company with a strong cultural foundation. And the evidence is irrefutable that a strong culture leads to superior performance, higher employee retention, and a better-aligned organization. Equally important, a strong culture driven by a handful of rules (core values) makes leading people much easier, reduces the need for stacks of policies and procedures, gives everyone a foundation from which to make tough decisions, and generally brings simplicity and clarity to many of these "people" systems within a firm. This chapter provides a simple exercise for discovering your core values if they've not yet been delineated, and eight actions for bringing your core values alive. You'll see how to use your core values to replace a number of random lists for organizing employee orientation, recruiting, interviewing, and performance management. In addition, using the Individual Performance Plan sheet structures an effective performance appraisal process around a firm's core values.

In building Verifone from $30 million to $600 million to dominate the global market of clearing credit card transactions, Hatim Tyabji said his key leadership and management tool was a booklet that explained, in eight languages, the eight core values at the heart of

Verifone's success. "I essentially spent the last six years repeating myself," noted Tyabji, as he built a strong, global culture on the foundation of these eight rules.

Finding the Right Words: Mission to Mars

If you already have your core values articulated, skip to the next section For those who haven't, read on. If you go at it cold, with a blank sheet of paper, figuring out your company's core values can be a frustrating and fruitless process. I've seen firms spend tens of thousands of dollars and several months going through a laborious discovery process, only to come away with a generic list that misses the uniqueness and power of the existing culture. Alternatively, there is a way to get at your core values that's fun and amazingly fast. It's an approach first suggested by Jim Collins. Using the method I'm about to describe, companies can get a good first draft of their core values in 15 minutes, a finished document in an hour. I refer to the process as the Mission to Mars.

Gather a representative group of employees or managers from across the company, or if you'd rather, your senior management team. Ask the group to pretend there's a team of Martian anthropologists studying American business, and they're trying to understand your company's corporate culture. Each individual is to come up with the names of five employees—ones who aren't in the room—to send to Mars. (Note: If you're a start-up and your list has to be the four or five initial founders or employees, that's fine.) The Martians don't speak English, and they don't know what a good PowerPoint presentation is, so whatever the Martians learn will have to come through observation. Given that, which five employees would best convey the good things about your company, just through their actions? Don't choose people because they know how to present well, nor eliminate someone because I mentioned this. Don't over-engineer by choosing a balanced team that represents each function in the business. Just choose the five who would best give the Martians a sense of what's good about the company.

When each individual has five names—no more, no less—go around the room and determine the top three vote getters. Important side note: Don't let these lists out of the room. This is simply a thought experiment and the conversations around the three individuals chosen should stay in the room. Starting with the employee who received the most mentions, initiate a conversation about these people. Who are they? How do they go about their work? What would customers or co-workers say about them? Why are they important or valuable to the organization? Another approach is to go the opposite direction—ask people to recall employees who didn't work out and brainstorm about what went wrong.

As you jot down what's being said, you'll begin to see themes and patterns emerge. Don't be surprised if the words that pop up are less polished or humanitarian than you might have hoped, and for Pete's sake, don't squelch those who utter them! Your goal is to know what the real core values of your organization are, not the Chamber of Commerce's notion of what they should be. Here's what Collins says about it:

> "...there is no universally right set of core values. A company need not have as its core value customer service (Sony doesn't) or respect for the individual (Disney doesn't) or quality (Wal-Mart Stores doesn't) or market focus (HP doesn't) or teamwork (Nordstrom doesn't). A company might have operating practices and business strategies around those qualities without having them at the essence of its being. Furthermore, great companies need not have likable or humanistic core values, although many do. The key is not what core values an organization has but that it has core values at all."

As you get closer to finding the right words and ideas to describe your company's core values, the energy level of the room will begin to rise. How will you know you've arrived? The goose bumps on your arm will tell you. You'll recognize your company's core values when you hear your employees stating some of your own deepest beliefs and motivations as their own. Then it takes little more than some word-smithing to get the concepts hammered into key words and rules that you can use. At Gazelles, we have six:

1. Practice What We Preach
2. Ecstatic Customers
3. 1st Class for Less
4. Honor Intellectual Capitalists
5. Everyone an Entrepreneur
6. Never, Ever, Ever Give Up

The Mission to Mars exercise is always powerful and revealing. I remember working through it with one of the companies in our Master of Business Dynamics program. The CEO had brought a relatively large management group to the meeting; there were probably 14 people around his table, out of the 120 total employees. The group quickly selected its five emissaries, but most of the proposed core values they put up on the board left the CEO restless. That is, until three words came into play: build, elegance, and design. You could see the synapses firing in this young CEO's brain. The word "build" took him back to his childhood, to working on projects with his dad, and it so happens that his company today provides software solutions to the construction industry. "Elegance" and "design" spoke to the impatience his employees know so well when he's confronted with a solution that seems clunky. The words resonated for him, and he seemed touched to know that they also rang true for his management.

What happened to that software company on that day was important for its future, and that's because the communication went both ways. His managers demonstrated that they knew the words that motivated their CEO, and the CEO gave them additional information with which to understand the deeper meaning of those words. Is it important for an organization and its CEO to understand one another in this way? Yes, absolutely. If the organization doesn't understand and starts to drift, the CEO loses his edge—maybe even gives up and sells. If the organization does understand, however, alignment happens and the company thrives.

Techniques for Bringing Your Core Values Alive

Once you have your values, the other 99 percent of the effort goes into keeping these values alive with existing employees and inculcating (bringing into the culture) new employees and acquisitions as they join the firm. It's the repeating of and living consistent with the firm's values that's the most difficult part of the process. A leader must go beyond merely posting the values on the wall and handing out plastic laminated cards. To keep things fresh, you have to get a little creative. You have to find lots of different ways to deliver the same information—over and over—so that it doesn't get stale, yet is reinforced on a daily basis.

Storytelling

Everybody enjoys a good story and most great leaders teach through parables or storytelling. While this provides that spoonful of sugar that helps the medicine go down, there's more to it than that. As I saw when I did the Mission to Mars exercise with my MBD client, a little bit of story and legend helps cement the bond between the CEO and employee. It keeps the CEO interested and involved. Above all, the story provides the explanation for any core values that might seem unusual or cryptic on their own. You can tell the story and, instead of offering a moral, you can say "and that's why we consider (blank) one of our core values."

The Mission to Mars exercise is an ideal time to start a tradition of corporate storytelling, but don't stop there. Incorporate storytelling wherever it logically fits into your management strategy. Tell the oldest stories when you can, but also encourage the telling of new stories. The more that employees are able to attach core values to incidents in their working lives, the more relevant and useful those core values become.

To get storytelling into your routine, start by making it a practice at your monthly or quarterly all-employee meetings (you do have them, don't you?) by sharing a story from the past month or quarter that represents each core value. The quickest way to come up with these stories is to take 15 minutes at one of your weekly executive-team meetings (you do have those, don't you?) and ask for nominations and examples. If you're among those who haven't yet established a routine of having all-employee and executive-team meetings regularly, read Chapter 8, Mastering the Daily and Weekly Executive Meeting.

Recruitment and Selection

Once you've established the words, rules, and stories that constitute your core values, put them to work in the recruitment and selection of employees. It's critical for new employees to feel comfortable in your culture, and the best way to determine that is to ensure that they align with your core values. Start by using the language from your core values in recruitment ads and job descriptions. This will catch the attention of those people who resonate with those values. When it comes time to interview, design several of your questions and assessments to test the candidates' alignment with your core values. For instance, we look for people with an entrepreneurial background (Everyone an Entrepreneur) and we ask for examples where they were faced with an almost insurmountable challenge and how they dealt with the situation (Never, Ever, Ever Give Up). Then, when it comes time to make a selection, have the various interviewers involved rate the candidate in terms of his or her perceived alignment with each core value. Your goal, after all, is to make sure your new hires fit in. The way to improve the chances of their fitting in is by making judgments about their ability to adopt your core values as their own.

Orientation

Once hired, it's time to inculcate the individual. Like many social organization initiations, orientation (you do have one, don't you?) is when you can further emphasize the company's core values.

Courtney Dickinson, formerly Sapient's Culture Architect, helped establish a week-long Boot Camp, in which a primary goal was to assist computer-trained techies to function in a customer-supportive environment. She used Sapient's core values to organize the experiential learning, and she found it uncommonly powerful. "I wish I had these core values to show my former employer, so they'd know why I left," one employee told her, "because this is what I believe." Dickinson says Boot Camp was optional at first—but not for long. "Just about everybody who didn't do Boot Camp was soon gone," she recalls. "It had a huge impact on retention."

At a minimum, have the CEO or other top executive come into orientation and share a company legend behind each core value. This will be reinforcing for all concerned.

Performance Appraisal

Just as core values should be the outline for your selection and orientation process, they should also be the skeleton on which you hang your performance-appraisal system. With a little creativity, any performance measure can be made to link with a core value. To get you started, I've included a sample Individual Performance Plan worksheet *(Figure 4-1)*. You can go to the Gazelles.com Website and download an editable blank worksheet.

Figure 4-1

Creating a Personal Plan

Overview and Instructions

The Planning Pyramid will serve as your strategic planning tool. In order to ensure that the very important things your company identified on its pyramid are accomplished, you'll need to be able to draw information from it and translate that into your Personal Plan for the next ninety days. We strongly recommend that you create one of these plans every ninety days.

Read through the sample plan below and then fill out your own.

Sample Personal Plan

Organization:_____ Name:_____

Core Values	Critical # / Theme
1. **Practice what we preach**	1. **80% ecstatic customers**
I will *ensure we all call at least one customer every week.*	1 will *use 360° review process to measure*
2. **Ecstatic Customers**	2. **Operation Transition**
I will *complete 100% of implementation process for every customer.*	1 will *move coaching responsibilities to Dan.*
3. **1st class quality for less**	**Brand Promise**
I will *reduce printing, books & shipping costs 20%.*	1. **"Ideas to Implementation"**
4. **Honor intellectual capitalists**	1 will *create standardized implementation kits for each MBD workshop.*
I will *create 1-page description of first three practices for yr. 2000.*	**Other Accountabilities** (Rocks, Key Initiatives)
5. **Never give up**	1. **Coach of coaches working**
I will *not give up on employees— coach to improved performance.*	1 will *prepare Dan to handle all processes himself.*
6. **Everyone an entrepreneur**	2. **Payment process**
I will *do what it takes to keep my 2 key clients happy.*	1 will *include prompt payment of deposit as part of successful implementation.*

In addition, organize your employee handbook into sections around each core value. In essence, these are the equivalent of the Ten Commandments around which all other guidelines should organize.

Recognition and Reward

When you're looking for recognition and reward categories, look no further than your core values. Using them publicly—at quarterly or annual meetings or on a good-news bulletin board—reinforces the primacy of these core values within your organization. You also gain a new source of corporate stories and legends each time a reward or recognition is given that highlights a core value. For instance, at our quarterly planning session we'll often recognize someone who exemplified the "1st Class for Less" or "Never, Ever, Ever Give Up" core value.

Internal Newsletter

Why struggle to come up with a catchy title for a newsletter when some word or phrase from your core values will do beautifully? Why organize your newsletter around seasons or quarters or heaven-knows-what, when you've got built-in themes in your core values? Highlight a core value with each issue, incorporating stories—yes, more stories—about people putting these core values to work for the betterment of the company.

Themes

I know I'm starting to sound a bit like a broken record here, but your core values are the most obvious source of quarterly or annual themes. Use your core values to bring attention to your corporate improvement efforts. Milliken, the textile manufacturer, takes one of its six core values and makes it the theme for the quarter, asking all employees to focus on ways to improve the company around the theme. The Ritz-Carlton chain goes to the other extreme and high-lights one rule every day, in locations worldwide. In either case, a rhythm has been established that keeps the core values in sight and in mind simply by repetition. As part of that process, you might even ask your employees to audit the firm as to its alignment (or non-alignment) with a particular core value. Such an effort does far more than reinforce the core value—it can produce some very healthy and needed dialogue. That's the sort of thing that keeps core values from being just a list on the wall.

Everyday Management

I've found that managers and CEOs can repeat core values endlessly without it seeming ridiculous—so long as the core values they're using are relevant and meaningful to their employees. When you make a decision, relate it to a core value. When you reprimand or praise, refer to a core value. When customer issues arise, by all means compare the situation to the ideal represented by the core values. The same goes for employee beefs and concerns—weigh them against your company's core values. Small as these actions may sound, they probably do more than any of the aforementioned strategies for bringing core values alive in your organization.

Have a Few Rules, Repeat Yourself, and Be Consistent

As you move forward discovering and bringing alive your core values, remember: this is no different than teaching your two-year-old right from wrong. Young, old, or in-between: people need to know what marks they're supposed to be hitting. They want to understand how they can conduct themselves to please you and your customers. They appreciate a reminder when they goof up. And they want to know the rules aren't a moving target or prone to selective enforcement. Your core values will do all of that for you, if you take the time to find out what they are and how you can best make use of them.

Now, in a growing environment, it may be tempting to say, "We don't have time to slow down and figure out things like core values!" But I've coached scores of companies over the years and I'll tell you, every company on a rocket, every company that's gaining sales and influence in quantum leaps, takes the time.

Core Value Checklist

ACTIVITY: In this column, list someone **accountable** for taking action on each item you want to pursue. Also, go to One-Page Strategic Plan and fill out Core Value column.

Have a few rules, repeat yourself, and be consistent.

Create Legends—Link a company story with each core value to make it memorable. Storytelling is the best way to teach. Do this now, while you're together.

Recruitment and Selection—Use the core values in your ads and selection process. Have them serve as the section themes or headings for your structured interview process.

Orientation—Have your core values serve as the major themes for your orientation process.

Appraisal Process—Have your core values serve as the section headings for your appraisal process. With a little creativity, any performance measure can be made to link with a core value.

Recognition and Reward—At the quarterly or annual company gathering, if you're looking for recognition and reward categories, look no further than your core values. And this serves to generate new stories to bring them alive.

Internal Newsletter—Each issue, highlight a core value with an example of someone exemplifying the value.

Themes—Whether as a theme for a particular round of good news stories or as a company-wide quarterly theme, use the core values to bring focus to improvement efforts. Ask people to take time to audit the firm along the lines of a core value. It produces some very healthy and often dialogue that is often needed, and needed often.

Everyday Management—Without going to the ridiculous (though it's hard to repeat yourself enough), relate decisions, reprimands, praise, customer issues, and employee concerns back to the core values. These daily actions will do more than any of the other strategies to strengthen the culture within the firm.

5

MASTERING ORGANIZATIONAL ALIGNMENT AND FOCUS

Know your top priorities!

Executive summary: The old saw is true: The organization with too many priorities has no priorities. This chapter will emphasize the need for management to clearly articulate to employees the five most important priorities that must be addressed or achieved to move the company to the next level. It's then critical that everyone in the organization determine his or her own Top 5 priorities, aligning them with the company's, and creating the clarity that's crucial for top performance. A Management Accountability Plan (MAP) aligns the specific activities with those priorities. In addition, this chapter will emphasize the need for additional clarity around the Top 1 of 5—the number-one priority that supersedes all others. A set of guidelines at the end of this chapter will help challenge you to determine your true Top 1 priority.

Have you ever noticed the lengths to which we human beings will go to avoid doing what needs to be done? There's no better time for cleaning the office than just before a big project or presentation is due. And who better to begin organizing the family photo album than the person who was supposed to be bringing order to the hall closet? It's just the way we are. We put lots of energy into avoiding the hard, unpleasant, realities of life. It's not that we don't know what to do. It's that we don't do it. This chapter emphasizes management's need to clearly articulate to employees the five most important priorities that must be addressed or achieved to move the company to the next level. It's then critical that everyone in the organization determine his or her own Top 5 priorities, aligning them with the company's and creating the activity plan that's crucial for top performance.

Management consultant Ivy Lee visited Bethlehem Steel Company decades ago, long before it became the world's largest independent steel producer. "With our services, you'll know how to manage better," said Lee to CEO Charles Schwab. Schwab grew indignant. "What we need around here is not more knowing, but more doing! If you'll pep us up to do the things we already know we ought to do, I'll gladly pay you anything you ask."

Lee took him up on the proposition. "In 20 minutes," he told Schwab, "I'll show you how to get your organization doing at least 50 percent more." He started by having Schwab write down and prioritize his six most important tasks to complete in the next business day. Then he told Schwab, "Put the list in your pocket and take it out tomorrow and start working on number one. Look at that item every 15 minutes until it's done. Then move on to the next, and the next. Don't be concerned if you've only finished two or three, or even one, by quitting time. You'll be working on the most important ones, and the others can wait."

The consultant encouraged Schwab to share this approach with his executives, judge its value, and "send me a check for whatever you think it's worth." Two weeks later, Lee received a check for $25,000—a king's ransom in those days. In an accompanying note, Schwab said it was the most profitable lesson he'd ever learned. The lesson, of course, was the power of focus. The organization that understands—and acts upon—its Top 5 and Top 1 of 5 is the organization that progresses and prevails.

Establishing a Planning Context for Your Top 5 and Top 1 of 5

In Chapter 3, the Planning Pyramid worksheet helped you align long-term goals with the quarterly challenges your organization faces. With these planning efforts in front of you, it's not hard to start figuring out what your Top 5 and Top 1 of 5 should be for the shorter term. Begin by asking yourself, what do I need to be doing *today* to keep this company moving towards its plans at the speed the market demands? Keep in mind your time frame, because these aren't necessarily annual priorities you're setting. Again, if you're growing 20–50 percent per year, a quarter equals a year. North of 100 percent growth, a month acts like a year.

Once you've determined your company's Top 5 and Top 1 of 5, each of your executives must determine his or her Top 5 and Top 1 of 5. Make the list the basis of a regular performance appraisal process. Continue to cascade this down the organization until you reach everyone. As you bring the process deeper into the organization and ratify it through the performance appraisal system, you're creating something magical called alignment. When you have everybody aligned, everybody at every level sees what you see and aspires to what you aspire. It's often helpful to hold a monthly or quarterly meeting of all your employees to review the firm's Top 5 and Top 1 of 5 priorities. Along with your core values, these priorities become the "handful of rules" that should drive decisions the next quarter. (Concrete tools for holding a successful quarterly meeting and driving quarterly priorities are provided in Chapter 6 Mastering the Quarterly Theme.)

But, to make your Top 5 and Top 1 of 5 something more than words on paper, to transform them into something achievable, you need a Management Accountability Plan or MAP *(Figure 5-1)*. Using this worksheet, you can assign the accountabilities necessary to get the job done. You can also download this worksheet from www.gazelles.com. Don't dawdle on this. Within 24 to 48 hours of establishing your Top 5 and Top 1 of 5, determine who's going to be the point person on what, and when they'll produce the deliverables. We're talking accountabilities, sub-accountabilities, resource needs, deadlines, and sub-deadlines. It all goes in the Management Accountability Plan. Fill it out carefully and the result will be a week-by-week strategic plan over 13 weeks, detailing the steps that need to be taken and the milestones that must be reached to complete or make progress with this priority. Again, cascade this process down your organization, requiring everyone to produce a one page MAP for each of their major priorities.

Straightforward enough, right? Well, it isn't necessarily. Identifying and pursuing your Top 5 and Top 1 of 5 can be difficult and downright

Figure 5-1

M.A.P.
Management Accountability Plan

Management Team Member: _____

"Big Rock": _____

Goal Title: _____

Story: _____
_____
_____
_____

	Actions	Who	When	Resources Needed
1st Qtr.				
2nd Qtr.				
3rd Qtr.				
4th Qtr.				
Next Year				
The Year After				

painful. If the process isn't at least making you uncomfortable, you probably haven't zeroed in on the right set of priorities, particularly your number one priority. We'll explore this subject next.

Recognizing Your Top 1 of 5: It's the One that Hurts

Perhaps the most outstanding recent example of how hard it can be to face and push through your Top 1 priority is golfer Tiger Woods. After winning the Masters, he was golf's golden boy—huge endorsement contracts and lots of press hype. Then he started losing, with people calling him a flash in the pan. For more than a year, he inexplicably failed to win anything. But now he's unstoppable, and Tiger has revealed to the world why. Tiger Woods had spent a long and agonizing year re-learning how to swing the club. He had realized that he would never achieve his goal of being golf's all-time greatest if he didn't adjust his swing, his number one and most difficult priority. For a while, the results were disastrous, but he endured. Tiger Woods had taken an unblinking look at himself and saw what was lacking. He recognized his Top 1 of 5, and he did what was required to face reality and push through the pain.

Seven Sore Points for Companies

In this last section of the chapter, I'll share with you seven common leading priorities and talk about how some companies I've worked with have addressed each. You'll find all seven in the Top 1 worksheet at the end of this chapter. You might want to keep a copy handy for easy reference.

Not big enough to compete

Often bigger is better. We have a manufacturing client that worked hard to improve its processes, respond to customer needs, build a great corporate culture, etc.—and each day the CEO knew in his heart he was sending his people up the hill to get slaughtered. He had a 10-ton gorilla of a competitor, and it was very clear to this leader that, long-term, the gorilla was going to win. As hard as this guy's people worked, all of his company's efforts would vaporize once the competitor threw money or manpower at the issue.

Reluctantly, this CEO acknowledged that it was never going to get any easier—until he himself became a 10-ton gorilla. He needed to merge with a bigger company.

My client sat, gave some thought to what might attract a buyer, and it became clear; he had to be the first in his industry to go to the World Wide Web with a solution. With that goal in mind—no small one, mind you—my client completely cleared his plate. For a year he did nothing but work with a programmer to get his company on the Web while the rest of his executive team ran the company. He built what became his industry's hottest trading site. And he reeled in the big fish he was looking for. He was able to successfully sell his firm to a 100-ton gorilla that made his competitor look like the small company his was before. This guy clearly recognized his number one priority, did what it took to complete it, and it paid off.

The company lacks a key player

One of the most danced-around issues in growing companies is personnel. How many times have we seen a company outgrow longtime players, yet instead of making the necessary personnel changes to strengthen their areas of responsibility, the CEO just starts growing redundant bureaucracy around the deadwood? It happens a lot and it holds a company back. Make replacing those people your number one priority now.

Perhaps the CEO wears too many hats. One firm I worked with desperately needed a CFO, but the founder-CEO just couldn't bring himself to pay the necessary salary to bring in a qualified financial person. He preferred to stretch himself too thin, and the company's results showed it. Once a CFO was on board, the company returned to growth and profitability within months.

The last version I'll cite to you is perhaps the toughest one of all: the need to replace yourself. We all know that the skills required to start a company aren't the same ones required to run and expand a company. Even Bill Gates reached this conclusion. At a certain point, he recognized that Microsoft would most benefit from getting him back to the visionary, entrepreneurial role he plays best. "Let [Steve] Ballmer be CEO," may have been the four smartest words Gates ever said.

The economic engine is broken

Maybe you're in a stupid business. Maybe the economic model on which you founded the company no longer makes sense. Whatever: you just know that the company is never going to make any money and you're surely not going to make it up in volume. The venture capitalists call it a "living-dead" company, meaning it's good enough to survive, but it's never going to do great things. Time to get out.

Don't read on too fast! Even if you're thinking, "My company's not a living-dead company," stop and consider: Are there parts of your company, or products, that meet the definition? Again, the advice is simple: Get out. Make that tough decision.

Someone else is controlling our destiny

It happens, unfortunately. Somebody gains control over a key component of your business. If it's not curtains for the company, it's certainly a crisis. When Netscape lost AOL and a couple of other key relationships to Microsoft, it tubed Netscape. The same thing happened to Donald Burr at PeopleExpress, the mid-eighties discount airline. When American Airlines developed the Sabre reservation system, and PeopleExpress couldn't keep up with the multi-tier structure, Burr found himself out of business four months later. The lesson is clear: If a competitor gets hold of a key relationship or patent or supply line, you'd better have a good counter-move or you're in trouble. I'll talk more about this in Chapter 7, which has to do with brand promises and controlling the choke point of your industry.

We need a war chest to compete

It's what you might call the FedEx dilemma. You just can't be a player in some industries unless you charge off the blocks fast and strong. I know the CEO of a startup telecommunications company who understood this well. Knowing his company wouldn't continue to exist unless it very quickly grew to scale, this guy spent just about all of his waking hours for several months amassing capital. His work culminated in a $210-million financing deal that got him the war chest he needed to compete. It's often one of the best reasons to go public.

We can't raise money 'til we grow

On the flipside, here's a cautionary tale to keep in mind when seeking capital. One of our MBD companies was adamant that its Top 1 of 5 was the need to raise $10 million. The executive team devoted itself to the goal—which is good. But the execs also took their eyes off the operational ball—which is bad. The result? Flat sales for two quarters. The company's valuation sagged badly, and would-be investors headed for the hills.

The CEO made the tough decision to forget about raising money and focus on driving up sales. He made everybody a salesperson, including himself and the CFO who was working on the fundraising front. For a solid three months, he had the executive team meeting daily and weekly in a war room setting to track progress. At the end of 90 days, the company posted a 40-percent increase in sales. That performance allowed the CEO and CFO to go out and resume raising money—this time at a much better valuation.

We've got to scale back or we won't survive

Here's another true story from our MBD files. For the first several years of a retail mortgage company's existence, the CEO considered his Top 1 of 5 to be rapid expansion—more markets, more mortgage products, more locations, more people. Then one day a large segment of his industry collapsed, due to various structural changes. It was gone. The only reason that company is around today, several years later, is because this CEO made the immediate and wrenching decision to lay off 240 of his 300 people. For quite a while, he looked like a failure. But his willingness to retrench got him back to the break-even point, and it kept his company alive long enough to see his industry move forward again. Often CEOs aren't willing to make the necessary cuts fast and deep enough. Instead, the death is slow and painful.

All of these examples prove one thing that Tiger Woods can vouch for with confidence: Pursuing your Top 1 of 5 goal is probably the most distasteful, frustrating, and perhaps discouraging thing you'll ever confront. It's not something you'll take on lightly, and I'd advise you not to do it alone. Tiger needed the clear-eyed advice and support of his coach, Butch Harmon. You need similar wisdom and backing from a strong board member or a mentor. But you'll be glad you made the effort. And your employees and investors will praise your gutsy leadership.

Top 1

What is your number one?

1. Simply not big enough to compete—need to merge with larger firm.

2. Lacking a key player—until this position is filled, a lot of other efforts are wasted.

3. Economic engine is broken—there is simply no way to make money given the way we're doing business.

4. Someone else is controlling our destiny—We've lost control of a key component of our business to a competitor.

5. We need $200-million war chest to get to a competitive scale.

6. Can't raise money until we get back on a growth path.

7. Must scale back rapidly to reach the break-even point and take another run at it.

6

MASTERING THE QUARTERLY THEME

Establish a reason to celebrate!

Executive summary: A company's goals and priorities won't be successful in driving the organization if they're easily forgotten or ignored. Once you've established what's important for your workforce to accomplish in the next quarter or year, you've got to do something to help your associates make the necessary emotional connection that generates commitment. Through a variety of real-world examples, this chapter will help you create the necessary themes and images to bring any corporate campaign to life. You'll also learn how companies track progress and celebrate success. Finally, you'll gain access to two tools that will assist you in planning theme-related events that will reach the myriad employees you have to lead and inspire.

What separates a plan on paper from one that lives and breathes on its own? It's an idea, an image—in short, an organizing theme. That's what transforms a mere managerial goal into a company-wide mission. This chapter will help you create the necessary themes and images to bring any corporate campaign to life. You'll also learn how companies track progress and celebrate success.

Great leaders have always understood the power of a theme. The Revolutionary War was organized around "No Taxation Without Representation!" and the Boston Tea Party became not just an event, but an enduring symbol. Martin Luther King Jr. built his goal of a more just society around his "I Have A Dream" speech. Visionaries

63

intuitively understand what too many business executives have yet to learn, which is that it takes an idea or an image to anchor a message with its listening audience. To get people to storm the barricades on your behalf, you've got to give them a concept that connects not just with their heads but with their hearts.

This need to connect with the feelings and desires of your workforce is proven and well accepted. In their seminal book, *The Leadership Challenge,* authors Jim Kouzes and Barry Posner speak powerfully of the need for CEOs to "encourage the heart" when seeking organizational alignment. I've seen it in action. I witnessed Michael Dell of Dell Computer rally his troops against a challenge from Compaq. He didn't just declare war on Compaq; he made the whole office a war zone. He donned army fatigues, he strung camouflage netting throughout headquarters, and he addressed his sales and production squadrons as if briefing them for a mission of no return. Did it make a difference? How could it not have?

At about the same time, baby America Online was under attack by giant Microsoft. Then-President Ted Leonsis gathered his AOL workforce and unveiled a huge dinosaur named Microsoft. In the weeks that followed, the dinosaur moved around headquarters as a trophy for any office or division that had struck a blow against the dinosaur.

One more larger-than-life example: CEO Mark Moses of Platinum Capital in Irvine once rode an elephant into a company meeting. (Where do you think Doug Harrison got the idea I told you about in Chapter 1.) Why? Because he was launching an expansion campaign and he wanted his employees to "think big." To this day, the elephant image resonates at that company. It's symbolic of taking risks, making leaps, and pushing forward.

Using Priorities and Critical Numbers to Drive Your Theme

Good themes don't pop out of thin air. The most powerful are those anchored in quantitative goals—be they annual numbers for companies growing less than 15 percent per year, or quarterly numbers for companies whose growth rate is north of that. Refer back to your One-Page Strategic Plan. With plan in hand, take your top priority and align it with your Critical Number—that one key measurable that you want your organization to focus upon. Then brainstorm a theme to go with it. It ought to be something that will make the numbers memorable.

This doesn't have to be anything particularly grand. The CEO of one major company had his three major priorities—represented by three Critical Numbers—engraved into wristwatches that he passed out to his execs. Whenever they checked the hour, they were reminded of the goals and that time was passing. It was simple and effective. So was the Phillips Group's decision to hold a company-wide meeting out of the back of a truck parked at a loading dock. The theme for the quarter was operational excellence, so what better way to emphasize the unsung heroes of the operation than to have the meeting on their under-appreciated turf?

But if you can come up with a theme whose production values rival Cecil B. DeMille's, I say, go for it! The movie *Apollo 13* has served many firms well as an organizing theme, complete with the famous line "Failure is not an option." At Synergy Networks, CEO Mark Gordon wanted to drive quarterly profitability and he saw it improving in three stages. What's got three stages? A rocket, of course, so Gordon donned a rented spacesuit and flanked himself with a chart depicting the profitability goals as a three-stage rocket. As he exhorted his team to greatness, he tossed space-themed toys out into the audience.

One useful source of quarterly themes is your core values. Take one each quarter and use it to bring focus and improvement to a certain aspect of the business. It's an excellent way to audit the organization's culture and to reinforce the core values. And speaking of values, no matter what the theme for the quarter, it's useful to review the organization's core values at the quarterly meeting, relating each to the theme. In addition, if you're into employee and team recognition activities, there is no better category of awards than your core values.

However you choose to develop and present your theme, do it with your whole workforce in mind. Thanks to the work of Harvard psychologist Howard Gardner, we now understand that there are at least seven different forms of intelligence: Verbal/Linguistic, Visual/Spatial, Bodily/Kinesthetic, Musical/Rhythmic, Interpersonal, and Intrapersonal. Each comes with its own preferred way of learning. At the end of this chapter is a chart entitled "Multiple Intelligences Summary" detailing the traits common to each of these seven intelligences. When you plan a theme-related event, try to hit as many of these intelligences as possible. Include not just words and pictures, but sounds, smells, feelings, and opportunities to reason, figure, or relate.

Tracking Progress and Keeping Score

What makes a theme a mission rather than a mere event? Effective reinforcement does, and that can be achieved through publicly tracking progress and keeping score.

At Synergy Networks, Mark Gordon's three-stage rocket lost a stage each time one of his profitability goals was met. It was a visual reminder of both the goals and the theme. It didn't hurt employee attention span, either, that there was a payout for the workforce each time a stage fell away from the rocket.

For Sapp Bros. Leasing, a truck-leasing business striving for 100 new leases by St. Patrick's Day, the tracking method was a big poster featuring 100 shamrocks. Each time a new lease was signed, another shamrock would be numbered. Again, there was a monetary payout when the goal was reached.

Progress doesn't have to be numerically quantifiable to be real, however. Each time the dinosaur took up residence in a new department at AOL, employees knew the company had made inroads in its battle against Microsoft. It was their way of keeping score. In all cases, the symbol or scoreboard for the theme was highly visible. This isn't the time for 8.5" x 11" charts. Make them big, make them noticeable, make them memorable.

As you plan your visible tracking and scorekeeping, keep in mind this is an ideal opportunity to involve and engage some of the people who don't normally get involved in quarterly or annual goal achievement. At the trucking company, the shamrock chart was beautifully designed and executed by somebody in the front office with an artistic streak. Her efforts enhanced the experience for everybody, including herself. You have people in your organization that can do the same, and more. They're just waiting to be asked.

Rewarding and Celebrating

Reward is sometimes considered a dirty word. It's assumed that if there's a reward involved, it's somehow buying the workforce's participation. I don't see it that way. I think people need to know where they're going and they want to know when they've arrived. It's like reaching the last day of school. Remember how great that felt, taking the last test in the last class on the last day of school? If somebody gave you a gift to take home, that was wonderful, but the real rush was just getting to the end and knowing you'd done it. It's like that on the job, too. Nobody's going to turn down a hard-won bonus or prize, but that's just the frosting on the cake. The real reward is the sense of celebration that comes from reaching a goal and doing it together.

At McKinney Lumber in Alabama, retention was the goal. When retention reached one level, the management team hosted a hotdog roast. When it reached the next level, the fare was barbecued chicken. At the highest and final level, it was steaks for everybody, management team doing the cooking. Now, a free steak dinner is nice, but was it enough to buy the workforce's participation? Probably not. Dinner was provided to celebrate the achievement of a shared goal — and to mark the end of the quarterly campaign.

At Gorman's Business Interiors in Detroit, former CEO John Anderson devised Gormanopoly, a Monopoly-like game that gave teams points for "just about anything you could incentivize," as Anderson put it. There were points for profitability goals, for improved collection on receivables, for customer satisfaction, for health and fitness, for community service, you name it. The scoreboard consisted of three ships—one representing each team—moving across a board to the finish line. The reward, or celebration, would be a Caribbean cruise for each team that satisfied the goal criteria. All three made it in the first year the game was played and the company gladly footed the $32,000 cost of sending each employee and his or her guest on the trip. "It was a huge success," recalls Anderson. "Not only was it good for the organization, it got us good PR without a lot of promotion, customers got engaged in it and learned about our [corporate] culture, and it was a great recruiting tool, too."

Advertising and PR firm RMR and Associates used an all-inclusive trip to Montego Bay, Jamaica as its prize for its annual open-book management goal last year. CEO Robyn Sachs says, "How they earned it was by hitting a particular gross income number, $2.7 million in AGI. Well, we blew the number out. We got to $2.9 million and took about 50 people to Jamaica. It was great." She adds, "The goal gets people focused on the right things, but it's still just a game and it's fun. You get the whole company pulling together."

This year, Sachs' company is playing Stockopoly, "a stock-appreciation-rate scheme" as she calls it. The reward or goal this time is "cold, hard cash" and, although the game's going well, Sachs says she's a tad disappointed. "The Jamaica trip had more of an emotional pull on people than the money is having," she says. "I'm starting to see that the trip got people more excited."

Maybe the lesson in these examples goes right back to the Kouzes-Posner book, *The Leadership Challenge*. The trick in developing a successful quarterly theme isn't just coming up with a good idea or presenting it well or tracking progress effectively or even celebrating success well. It's encouraging the heart. Only when we do that extraordinarily well do we experience extraordinary success. At the end of this chapter is a worksheet you can use to organize your quarterly theme rollout.

Multiple Intelligences and the Quarterly Theme

Intelligence	Activities	Materials	Strategies	Presentation Skill
Verbal/Linguistic	lectures, discussions, word games, storytelling, choral reading, journal writing, etc.	books, tape recorders, typewriters, stamp sets, books on tape, etc.	read about it, write about it, talk about it, listen to it	teaching through storytelling
Logical/Mathematical	Brain teasers, problem solving, science experiments, mental calculation, number games, critical thinking, etc.	calculators, math manipulatives, science equipment, math games, etc.	quantify it, think critically about it, conceptualize it	Socratic questioning
Visual/Spatial	visual presentations, art activities, imagination games, mind-mapping, metaphor, visualization, etc.	graphs, maps, video, art materials, optical illusions, cameras, picture library, etc.	see it, draw it, visualize it, color it, mind-map it	drawing/mind-mapping concepts
Bodily/Kinesthetic	hands-on learning, drama, dance, sports that teach, tactile activities, relaxation exercises, etc.	building tools, clay, sports equipment, manipulatives, tactile learning resources, etc.	build it, act it out, touch it, get a "gut feeling" of it, dance it	using gestures/dramatic expressions
Musical/Rhythmic	superlearning, rapping, songs that teach	tape recorder, tape collection, musical instruments	sing it, rap it, listen to it	using voice rhythmically
Interpersonal	cooperative learning, peer tutoring, community involvement, social gatherings, simulations, etc.	board games, party supplies, props for role plays, etc.	teach it, collaborate on it, interact with respect to it	dynamically interacting, with participants
Intrapersonal	individualized instruction, independent study, options in course study, self-esteem building, etc.	self-checking materials, journals, materials for projects, etc.	connect it to your personal life, make choices with regard to it	bringing *feeling* into presentation

Quarterly Theme Meeting

Who's Accountable?

When will you hold the meeting?

Theme of Meeting?

Using the Multiple Intelligences list of activities, what will you do at the meeting?

Verbal/Linguistic

Logical/Mathematical

Visual/Spatial

Bodily/Kinesthetic

Musical/Rhythmic

Interpersonal

Intrapersonal

7

MASTERING EMPLOYEE FEEDBACK

De-hassle your organization!

Executive summary: Recurrent customer and employee hassles cost your employees 40 percent of their time, not to mention what it's costing your company in lost customers and revenues. You should construct a system of employee feedback to figure out which problems (opportunities in disguise) are arising and recurring in your organization or with your customers. At the end of the chapter is a six-point process your associates can use to resolve identified hassles. In addition, an important part of this feedback is objective daily and weekly measures that provide a sense of reality in terms of the future of the firm. Guidelines are provided for what these Smart Numbers and Critical Numbers should be.

What makes people hate their jobs? What makes them non-productive, complaint-happy deadwood? The answer: recurring problems and hassles. I'm talking about the situations, problems, and mistakes that happen over and over again, never getting fixed. Recurring problems and hassles are worse for customers, who don't have any incentive (like salary) to hang around.

Don't get me wrong: Humans like a challenge. When problems crop up in ones and twos, we gear up to perform. Struggling to a solution can be exhilarating, even affirming. Solving customer problems is at the heart of business and can actually build loyalty and lead to new opportunities. But recurring problems are something else entirely. They're like water on a rock, wearing your organization down day after day, leaving associates and customers frustrated.

Believe it or not, recurring problems eat up more than 40 percent of the average employee's time. 40%! Why so much? Because a problem is never just one person's problem. The person who discovers the glitch has to talk about it with not one person but several, and probably more than once. Fixing the problem, or even just putting a Band-Aid on it, means bringing progress to a screeching halt.

To reduce your costs, shorten your cycle time, and generally improve your internal working environment, you need to systematically gather data on what's hassling your employees—and then *do* something about it. And because your employees are often closest to the customer, their hassles are usually related to what's hassling your customers, giving you tremendous insight into ways to serve your customers better. Their hassles are your opportunities.

Two great managers have inspired me on this score. Jack Welch's Six Sigma Institute preaches the fundamentals of quality control, not just for quality's sake, but for profit's sake. When you get your process running at 99.997 percent of perfection—essentially hassle free—you get black-belt certification. Great process, great results, less hassles. But I didn't learn how simple yet powerful a de-hassling system of collecting employee and customer feedback could be until I met Michael Dell.

Almost two decades ago, when Dell Computer was just a baby called PCs Limited, Michael had his employees keeping weekly lists. He urged them to write down every problem, complaint, concern, issue, idea, or suggestion that had either crossed their minds or had been reported by a customer that week. On Thursday afternoons these lists were turned in, and Michael took them home to read and to search for the patterns and trends that would emerge over several weeks and months of collecting employee and customer concerns and suggestions. On Friday morning, he'd call everyone together for what became known as "the hour of horror." Employees would gather around and brainstorm solutions to some—but not all—of the problems.

Being selective was smart, because Michael Dell understood the concept of compound interest. He knew then, as my savviest clients do today, that if you solve just one percent of your problems or make a one percent improvement in your products and services each week, you'll gain greater and greater yields from the solutions with each passing year. If, on the other hand, you aim for solving too many problems, you'll have made a hassle out of your de-hassling system! Instead of being your key productivity-enhancing tool, it'll become just another drag on everybody's time.

Gathering the Data: Be Encouraging, Be Responsive

To get started, ask your employees a three-part question: What should we start doing, what should we stop doing, and what should we continue doing? Have them think about these questions from both their perspective and the perspective of customers. This initial survey will let people get things off their chests, especially if they haven't had the chance before. Compile the data, call a meeting, and brainstorm some solutions. Don't make it a chore; make it fun. Then, in your company newsletter (you do have one, don't you?), report progress on some of the stickier, long-term issues that have cropped up. That'll pave the way for introducing a more systematic ongoing process for collecting this feedback using a manual or electronic logging process.

This ongoing process encourages and requires your employees to log recurring problems they and your customers are experiencing. Suggest that you want to hear about anything and everything that caused them to spend more than a minute doing something that shouldn't have needed doing. What are customers requesting that can't be provided? Where are they being hassled in the process of doing business with your firm? You might even prime the pump by holding a weekly prize drawing, and offer a raffle ticket for each hassle submitted until the habit becomes established. To make it clear this isn't a top-down directive, make your own executive-level list to share: What are the top 10 things that make *your* job a hassle?

The key is to get the raw, unedited data. Even if a problem occurred and was resolved, it needs to be logged so patterns and trends can be observed. At the Ritz Carlton hotels, noted for winning two Malcolm Balridge awards for outstanding quality and service, personnel are required to log all incidences of customer or employee problems or concerns and turn them in daily to the general manager. This data points out opportunities for improvement that save time, improve working conditions, and increase customer delight.

Handling the Feedback

The trick to getting your de-hassling system humming is to be responsive. If employees feel their feedback is dropping into a black hole, it'll dry up. Initially, find some quick-hit solutions. If there needs to be a bigger wastebasket in the women's restroom, get a new one in there pronto. If there are bigger, thornier issues (I find they're usually related to IT or billing), put a team on one or two of them and schedule regular updates.

There's no way to predict how much hassle input you'll receive. You could get a lot; you could get a little. If your team is reluctant to provide feedback, don't shame them; just work extra hard to respond to the few items you receive. You'll get more participants next time, I promise. If, on the other hand, you find yourself swamped with input, don't give in to the temptation to omit items, combine them, or summarize them. Get the raw data out there even if the initial list numbers 1,784 items, as it did the first time I did this with a client over a decade ago. People are watching to see if their contributions are being considered. Again, don't summarize the data, give it back to the team in raw form. The only exception is if the feedback includes personal attacks. These should be dealt with privately.

Some companies handle long lists by posting them on a Website, or sending them out via e-mail. In Boston, a company called The Mathworks has established an internal online interest group where people can log and discuss their hassles. I've seen a few companies ask their employees to categorize their beefs by checking topic boxes, but remember: nobody should feel they've been summarized away.

Reporting Progress

People will want to see change as it's occurring. At Columbia University Business School some years ago, the dean posted a bulletin board for complaints and suggestions. Students and faculty alike knew they'd been heard when he scrawled on the notecards "Noted, done." Closing the loop in this fashion is absolutely crucial. Let people know what issues are being addressed, and which ones have been resolved. If it's something you can't do anything about, say more than that—*lots* more. When a customer bemoans the loss of a product at Sundance, a locally owned natural food store in Eugene, Oregon, management may devote a page to explaining the vicissitudes of dealing with distribution companies—and they'll post it for all to see, right next to the original complaint. People may not be pleased, but at least now they understand.

Some companies will even keep an issues-aging report, tracking how long an issue has been outstanding, so it doesn't fall through the cracks. One lumber firm in Alabama had a simple way to keep the issues "in sight, in mind." They wrote each issue on a large roll of paper and posted it on the factory wall where it stayed until it was resolved.

De-Hassling Etiquette 101

Now that I've sketched out an employee feedback system in broad strokes, let's spend a little time on the finer points. In the wrong hands, a de-hassling system can become an elaborate waste of time, or worse yet, a newfangled version of the old-fashioned corporate witch hunt. Don't let it happen to you. Use my six-point set of problem-solving guidelines (found at the end of the chapter) weekly, monthly, whatever—just to keep you on track.

The first three of my six guidelines have to do with getting your hassles under a microscope, checking them for relevancy and specificity, then making sure you're addressing the root of the issue. Why tackle one particular hassle if there are others that have greater impact on how your company works (relevancy)? Go after what's causing the most pain in the organization. Why gallop off to solve "communications problems" if you're not sure whether somebody's talking about facts or faxes (specificity)? Don't let people get away with saying "the system's always down." Find out when, where and what are the patterns. And are you sure you're not treating the symptoms instead of curing the disease (address the root)?

I remember surveying employees for a client in Tennessee. The number one issue was that "all the customers are mad" which was leading to the customers abusing the associates. Clearly this was a relevant issue. However, the use of the term "all" pointed out a need to get specifics. Looking further into the issues, we found that the warehouse was mis-shipping various items. We then turned to looking for the root of the problem. A key technique is asking "Why" several times. Why were items being mis-shipped? We discovered that the fifth copy of a five-part form was difficult to read. So why was it hard to read? Because the impact printer spitting out these picking forms had a worn-out impact print wheel (remember those days?). The point: many big problems trace back to simple solutions if you'll just get Colombo-like and ask a lot of questions. And along the way, someone might ask why the system needs five copies in the first place!

The remaining three guidelines on my six-point list have to do with keeping your de-hassling system fair and humane: focus on the process (the "what") and not the people (the "who"): involve all those affected; never backstab.

To avoid having the feedback degenerate into name-calling, focus on the what, not the who. When all the what's keep leading to the same who, of course, you may need to free up that person's future. And in that case, you still need to identify the "what" behind the failure of the "who" or you're destined to make the same hiring mistake. But that's rare. Most hassles are process hassles, not people hassles.

To save you the chore of running around to ten people and hearing ten different stories, be sure to involve all those affected. One of our major aircraft manufacturers found it could save a half-million dollars per jet, just by getting the whole team together to discuss problems instead of talking in smaller groups.

Finally, never backstab. We all have the right to face our accuser. Besides, we're more likely to get to the root of the problem when all those affected are in the same room and thus less likely to attack the "who."

With these guidelines in place, you'll ensure that your employee-feedback system raises morale instead of defeating it, and improves productivity, rather than sapping it.

Management-Development Opportunities

Surely by now you've thought, "Great, an employee feedback system. Another fine task to add to my already-bulging job description." But de-hassling your organization *doesn't* have to fall on the backs of the executive team. In fact, it's better to form a mid-management team to handle the initial screening and problem solving. Who else is as close to the action? Not you. Who better to know which items deserve priority attention and which employees are best suited to finding the solution? Again, probably not you. Think of it as a management-development opportunity, an investment in your eventual succession plan, as your supervisors and mid-managers have the opportunity to creatively address issues and improve performance and customer satisfaction.

Daily and Weekly Measures

The following sections will help you define what daily and weekly measures you and your company should focus on to drive performance, guide priorities, and help anticipate problems and opportunities. These measures will also help everyone in the company answer the fundamental question, "Did I have a good week?", which provides an objective indication of progress important to maintaining morale and enthusiasm.

Critical Numbers

It's best if the company has one or two Critical Numbers around which to align the company over the next quarter or year. A Critical Number represents a key short-term focus in the company that will have the most impact on the future of the firm. For instance, Dell Computer chose increasing the ratio of server sales to PC sales as their focus for 2001, knowing that this would focus the organization on transitioning from the PC market, which was slowing down in growth, to the faster-growth server market. Overall, the key question to ask is "What is the single most important measurable thing we need to accomplish in the next 3-to-12 months?" And I want to emphasize that this focus should change regularly to improve different aspects of the organization. It's like a weight lifter who focuses on different muscle groups during each workout to maintain proper proportions and to keep it interesting. It also lets different muscle groups rest.

Smart Numbers

Next, the executive team should identify three Smart Numbers that give them insight into how the company is likely to do in the future. The ability to predict is a key leadership function. A Smart Number is typically a complex ratio made up of key indicators like the ratio of sales this week against the same week last year compared to the growth rate of the market. This would tell you if you're really gaining market share or not. Or you might look at the ratio of sales calls made to those closed to give an indication of sales effectiveness. One CEO I met simply counted the number of trucks at the loading dock compared to the number of orders that week to know if it was going to be a good month next month. As the name implies, these key weekly measures make you smarter about how the business is doing. Once you've discovered three effective measures, you need to stick with them for a period of time so you can compare apples to apples.

Measures for Everyone

Once the Smart Numbers and Critical Numbers are decided, every person or team should have one or two daily or weekly measures that align with these numbers. The key is *alignment* or what Jack Stack, author of the *Great Game of Business,* calls "line of sight." Can every employee see how what they're doing impacts the entire firm? One organization chose improving their customer service rating as a Critical Number to focus on for one quarter. Based on this, every employee or team figured out something they could do better to improve this rating, from improving the speed of response, to accuracy of order taking, to timeliness of returning phone calls.

Highly Visible

Make your measurements visible. Like the standard six-foot tall United Way campaign barometer, your company-wide measurements—preferably in some graphical form—should be on large charts placed where the individual, team, or company can see the results. And I strongly suggest that every office employee has some kind of whiteboard in their cubicle or office on which to graph their own daily and weekly measures. These numbers have a much greater impact if people see them on a large graph. It is even better if they have to plot the numbers themselves. There's something powerful in having to physically plot the points and connect the dots on the graph to bring the results alive and make them personal. It's also useful to display last year's results on the graph along with a projected or budgeted target line.

Prediction

Once the habit of daily and weekly measuring is established, you want to start projecting ahead in addition to simply documenting the past. Jack Stack calls this Forward Forecasting. This involves making an educated guess about how the next few weeks or months are likely to turn out based on what you know now. Then, by comparing actual results against predicted results, you'll begin to learn how to better predict outcomes and strengthen your knowledge about what drives results for yourself, your team, and the company.

Situation Room

I recommend creating a situation room for the executive team. A situation room is where you display your core values and purpose, priorities for the quarter and year, and a map of the geographical territory you cover. Also display your Smart Numbers and Critical Numbers large and graphically. Make someone accountable for making sure the displays are up-to-date. If you do not have a separate room and you don't want visitors seeing your information, get an easel on wheels for about $300 that has a whiteboard on one side and a corkboard on the other. Use the whiteboard for general discussions and then, for your weekly executive team meeting, turn it around to show the corkboard side, where you have mounted all your maps, graphs, and lists. There are also reversible whiteboards that hang on the wall, or you can place the information behind a curtain along one end of the room. However, many firms proudly display this information even for customers to see, giving customers confidence that the firm is well managed and the executive team well informed.

Summary

In summary, it is absolutely essential that you develop daily and weekly measurements for the company, and daily and weekly measurements for every individual or team that align with the company measures. These numbers focus everyone's attention on driving performance, reinforcing priorities, and helping anticipate problems and opportunities. Make these measurements highly visible and graphical for everyone to see, and create a situation room for the executive team. Most importantly, just start measuring something and keep tracking different metrics until you find those that provide the most insight and useful feedback.

Problem-Solving Guidelines

You might note that these guidelines are similar to those found in conflict-resolution, decision-making, and problem-solving courses.

Relevancy—Does the issue really matter, is it of top importance, is there a customer affected by the hassle? Here you are looking for a pattern of recurring hassles. You can't solve every hassle right away, so you want to look at those that are costing customers and employees the most time or money.

Be Specific—Look back over your hassle lists. Did you write in generalities or list specifics? Some people will list as a hassle communications problems, or interruptions, or having to answer the same questions over and over. However, you can't begin to address these issues without knowing the who, what, when, where, how, and why of these hassles. Being specific also means being careful when using the words "always," "never," and "all the time." In staff meetings, push people to give specifics.

Address the Root—Look at the cause of the issue and not just the symptoms. Let's say you've identified a specific communications problem—in most cases, the standard response is "send out a memo." Rarely does this get to the root of the problem—instead, it serves as a quick fix. One of the best ways to get to the root of the problem is using the "5 Whys" technique. Ask "why" several times until you get to the root cause.

Focus on the *What*, Not the *Who*—You don't want to turn your search into a finger-pointing or blame game. Besides, 95 percent of the time, it's a process problem, not a people problem. However, if all the *what's* keep leading to the same *who*, maybe you've waited too long and the person has to be let go. But you should still ask "What did we do wrong that caused this person to fail?" Maybe your hiring or training process needs to be improved. If you don't get to the root of the *what*, you'll keep making the same *who* mistakes.

Involve All Those Affected—Rather than run around getting ten explanations from ten people, get them all in the same room to give a truer picture of the entire problem. Getting everyone in the room together also helps to minimize suboptimization—where fixing a problem in one part of the organization causes greater problems elsewhere.

Never Backstab—Never talk negatively about anyone if that person is not present. The only exception is if you need to seek the advice of someone before confronting the individual. In this case, you still need to bring the individual into the conversation as soon as possible. This guideline has its roots in such principles as the right to face your accuser and to be present when being judged. Besides, when you talk negatively about someone to another person, they have to then wonder if you are talking negatively about them behind their back. If you can be successful in implementing this rule, the level of trust and openness in your organization will improve immensely. And when the other person is present, everyone tends to follow the first five guidelines more closely.

8

MASTERING THE DAILY AND WEEKLY EXECUTIVE MEETING

Structure meetings to enhance executive team performance!

Executive summary: To make more than just a lot of noise in your business, you've got to have rhythm. And the faster you want to grow, the faster you have to pulse. At the heart of executive team performance is a rhythm of tightly run daily, weekly, monthly, quarterly, and annual huddles and meetings—all of which happen as scheduled, without fail, with specific agendas. With these meetings you'll have opportunities to focus your executives on what's important. You'll also solve problems more quickly and easily, you'll achieve better alignment around strategic decisions, and you'll communicate more effectively. This chapter will tell you who should be attending your meetings, what should be on the agendas, when the meetings should occur, who should run the meetings and how they should be run. I also highly recommend reading Patrick Lencioni's book *Death by Meeting*—it's a quick read.

Reading John D. Rockefeller's biography, *Titan,* I was struck by his daily luncheon habit. Each day, without fail, he'd sit down with his key people, have lunch, and talk. At first, the meetings included only Rockefeller and the four co-founders of Standard Oil. But as the decades wore on and the company grew, the meetings came

83

to include Rockefeller's nine directors. And yes, they continued to meet daily.

Consciously or not, Rockefeller understood that the word company meant "to share bread." He knew that by gathering his top lieutenants and advisors each day for a meal, their personal and professional relationships would be strengthened. Fortified for another day, each could go out and do his share to conquer the oil industry or Wall Street or whatever the current target might have been. Did it matter that the meetings occurred daily? I'm confident Rockefeller would say an emphatic "Yes!"

Meetings: A Routine to Set You Free

In the 19 years I've spent working with growing companies, the predictable winners are those who have established a rhythm and a routine of having meetings. The faster they're growing, the more meetings they have. This may sound ludicrous to those of you who have worked for large corporations, where meetings are dreaded interruptions that eat up hours or even days. But I'm not talking about the kind of wide-open, poorly defined meetings many of us have endured. I'm talking about short, punchy meetings with a structure, time limits, and a specific agenda. This type of meeting doesn't leave you feeling bogged down. On the contrary! This type of meeting routine actually sets you free.

Think about jazz for a minute. Lots of freedom in that, right? At first glance, all you see is the improvisation. But if you study jazz or talk about it with somebody who really knows the idiom, you soon realize that there is a rock-solid rhythm and a set of rules underlying all that passionate free-styling. To come together and create something amazing, all players must understand jazz's basic structure and agree to work within it. They have to know the key and the time signature. They have to establish how many bars are theirs for a solo (usually eight), and they need to know who to take the hand-off from. That's what separates hot music from noise.

For growing companies, when meetings are the rhythm and agendas are the rule, pros and unknowns can come together to create something new and marvelous. New people (and even newly acquired companies) get up to speed quickly when there's an obvious structure they can align with.

More Meetings, Not Less

Take a look at the meeting rhythm I'm advocating. Quarterly and annual meetings are givens in most companies. At the quarterly, you measure progress toward a year-end goal. At the annual, you consider that progress and set new goals for the following year. The key agenda for these quarterly and annual meetings is based around the One-Page Strategic Plan (described in Chapter 3). That's all well and good. But I am absolutely adamant that you need to add daily, weekly, and monthly meetings as well. Why? Because the agendas of these more-frequent meetings drive the deliverables outlined in the less-frequent meetings. Each one builds upon the next.

For example, how are you going to make your quarterly goals if you aren't driving performance monthly, weekly, even daily? Your execs need regular, face-to-face huddles to discuss new opportunities, strategic concerns and bottlenecks as they arise. Similarly, how many hours is it going to take to hammer out a set of goals for a new year, if the annual meeting is the first time anybody's talked about where the market's going or dealt with the tactical issues that come up weekly?

I want to make a side point here, and that is, the faster you're growing, the faster your meeting rhythm should pulse. In general, if you're growing less than 15 percent per year, you can treat the year like a year from a strategic thinking standpoint. If you're growing 20 percent to 100 percent a year, think of each *quarter* as if it were a year. That means plotting new strategy each quarter. If you're among the elite, more than doubling your revenue each year, you need to treat each *month* as if it were a year. For more discussion on this hyper-pulsing style of management, read the seminal book *Competing on Internet Time* by Michael Cusumano and David Yoffie. It outlines the browser battle between Netscape and Microsoft. Netscape sustained rapid and successful growth by treating each month as if it were a year. Growing faster than almost any firm at the time, Netscape nonetheless took its executives offsite each and every month to hold a formal strategic meeting. In so doing, Netscape didn't just talk the talk of pulsing monthly; they walked it.

Daily Meeting—An Imperative

Absolutely everybody in a growing company should be in some kind of five- to 15-minute huddle *daily*. I don't mean they all have to be in the same meeting, just in some meeting. To me, this is non-negotiable.

Of course, the immediate pushback I always get on this is, "We're too busy!" People moan and groan about how thinly they're spread, or how much they're traveling. They can't imagine finding the time to get everybody in the same place every day for 1 minute, let alone 5 or 15. Or, if the company is quite small and travel isn't that big an issue, they'll tell me, "We don't need a meeting when we're seeing each other all day long."

Each argument sinks of its own weight. First off, thank goodness for cell phones. The meeting doesn't have to be in your conference room or around somebody's desk. A conference call or a speakerphone session will do just fine when people are on the road. And what's 5 or 15 minutes? The equivalent of a bathroom break! Second, this stuff about working too hard or seeing each other too much already is besides the point. Casual encounters fail to take advantage of the three most powerful tools a leader has in getting team performance: peer pressure, collective intelligence, and clear communication. I'll elaborate a little right now; more later in the chapter.

The meetings I'm talking about save you time. By maintaining a rigorous daily meeting schedule, you'll always be able to find one another for a substantive consultation. If you need an answer to a customer question, you don't need to say, "I'll try to find her and get back to you sometime today." You can name the time, because you know you'll have the answer by the end of your daily meeting. Nor will you be going over the same water-cooler conversation three or four times, as is the case when you rely on chance hallway meetings for communication. Because everyone's together in a daily meeting, things get quickly and accurately communicated. No more "telephone game," where the message changes as it gets passed along.

Equally important, in one-on-one meetings there is a lot of private negotiating going on ("You know what I'm up against...."), putting the leader in the constant position of being the bad guy. However, by having everyone on the same call for a few minutes, it takes the heat off the leader and provides peer pressure that increases the rate of deliverables.

Last, a daily meeting focuses the collective intelligence of the team on the issues at hand. What a shame to have a high-powered exec team that doesn't take even 15 minutes each day or an hour a week to focus its horsepower on the opportunities at hand! Without the discipline I'm describing, don't kid yourself into thinking you're getting this focused attention.

Timing

To work well, the daily meeting must be set up right. I recommend that companies set the time a little irregularly—every day at 8:08 a.m., for example, or every day at 4:46 p.m. For whatever reason, people do a better job of being on time when the time's not on the half or quarter-hour. Worried that you'll forget the meeting? I use iping.com which pages or phones you to remind you of the meeting for a nominal cost.

Make on-time attendance mandatory, with no excuses! I've been in intense meetings with clients. I've been in the midst of seeking funds from venture capitalists. It doesn't matter; I tell them I need to take a break for my daily meeting. And it only gains me respect.

Overall, start and end on time and don't problem solve. This meeting is simply for problem identification. And if it starts to go longer than 15 minutes, people will drop the habit.

Setting

Meet wherever you want, but I strongly suggest you avoid sitting comfortably. Stand up, or perch on stools. It'll help keep the meeting short. Gathering in the leader's office makes it easier for him or her. If via conference call, there are a lot of affordable services today given the revolutions in telecommunications.

Who Attends

The general rule is, the more the merrier—though you may wish to alter the approach a little if the group gets quite large or far-flung.

The Ritz Carlton gathers about 80 headquarters personnel for a ten-minute daily huddle outside the CEO's office. Also, in every Ritz hotel from Bali to Boston, each employee who isn't on the desk or answering phones attends a daily shift meeting to discuss problems and reinforce company philosophy. Marriott has continued the practice since purchasing the Ritz.

Alan Rudy at Express-Med uses daily huddles to keep his company pulsing, too. But, because he's got his people on multiple project teams, he's begun calling them all together for a single 15-minute meeting. For the first five minutes the project leaders report what's happening and describe any sticking points that have developed. After that, everybody huddles as needed. The beauty of Rudy's approach is that it gets absolutely everybody out of his or her cubicle and involved. Where once a project leader had to seek out somebody whose task overlapped his or her own, the inevitable redundancies and cross-functional needs now get worked out almost methodically.

Perhaps the most ambitious daily meeting schedule I know of belongs to The Scooter Store, a nationwide seller of motorized scooters, mainly for the elderly. The entire company re-aligns every 24 hours, through a rapid series of daily huddles. First, the frontline teams across the country huddle locally for 15 minutes. Immediately following that meeting, the leaders of those teams meet on a national conference call for another 15 minutes. Last, the executive team meets for a final 15-minute session. Across a mere 45 minutes each day, the entire company confers—bottom to top.

Who Runs the Meeting

Pick someone who is naturally structured and disciplined, (and that might not be the CEO). Whoever it is, the main job is to keep things running on time. Use a countdown stopwatch to make sure you don't let any part of the agenda run away with the meeting.

The person running the meeting also has the important job of saying, "Take it offline." Whenever two or more people get off on a tangent that doesn't require everybody's attention, instruct them to continue the conversation outside the boundaries of the meeting.

The Agenda

The agenda should be the same structure every day, and it's just three items long: what's up, daily measures, and where are you stuck? In the first five minutes, each attendee spends a few seconds (up to 30) just telling what's up. That alone is valuable, because it lets people immediately sense conflicts, crossed agendas, and missed opportunities.

Next, the entire group takes a quick look at whatever daily measurement your company uses to track its progress. (You do have one, don't you?) A dot-com company might track Website hits. A sales organization might track the number of proposals that went out that day. Wal-Mart uses stock price. Also, choose a short-term employee-based activity you want to focus on and track daily. Maybe it's accounts receivable, or getting contracts back on time. It ought to be some sort of measurable behavior.

The third and most important agenda item is where people are stuck. You're looking for bottlenecks, which ought to be your nemesis in business. Applying energy anywhere but the sticking point is a waste.

There are a couple of reasons why I consider this last part of the agenda crucial. First, there's something powerful in simply verbalizing—for the whole group to hear—your fear, your struggle, your concern. It's the first step to solving the problem, because until the mouth starts moving, the brain won't engage. Second, the bottleneck discussion often reveals who's not doing his or her job. Any time somebody goes two days without reporting a sticking point, you can bet there's a bigger problem lurking. Busy, productive people who are doing anything of consequence get stuck pretty regularly. The only people who don't get stuck are those who aren't doing anything. So, scrutinize the exec who reports, "Everything is fine!"

Important as it is, the bottleneck conversation shouldn't be allowed to drift into problem solving. It's okay if somebody wants to reply to a bottleneck by saying, "Call so-and-so," but anything more than that should be taken offline. Remember: The daily meeting needs to be kept short. At the end of this chapter is a one-page overview of the daily meeting agenda.

The Weekly Meeting Agenda

The weekly meeting has a different purpose, and therefore, a different agenda. It's intended to be a more issues-oriented and strategic gathering. It won't be, however, unless you've established your daily meeting rhythm. By holding daily meetings, you put out a lot of the fires and clear up a lot of the outstanding issues that would otherwise bog down weekly meeting. That's the all-important synergy.

In the paragraphs that follow, I'll discuss some of the differences between the daily and weekly meeting agendas. See the back of the chapter for a complete agenda for the weekly meeting.

The Schedule

Schedule the meeting for the same time, same place each week; 30 minutes for frontline employees and a full hour for execs. Again, it can be a conference call, as we do on Monday's at 5:05 p.m. EST, if your executives work in different locations.

Five Minutes: Good News

Each weekly meeting starts with five minutes of good-news stories from everyone. They could be personal or professional in nature, the more fun the better. Laughter brings brains into an alpha state, the result being more effective meetings. This starts the meeting on a good note, focuses everyone on the positive and serves as a mental health check. If someone has gone a couple weeks without specific good news, the leader should intervene privately to see if everything is okay.

Ten Minutes: The Numbers

Spend ten minutes on individual and company-wide measures of productivity. Every firm should have three key performance indicators that I call Smart Numbers. These are usually ratios that provide true insight into the future performance of the business. And these measures should be displayed graphically (see the weekly meeting agenda at the back of the chapter).

Ten Minutes: Customer and Employee Feedback

Spend the next ten minutes reviewing specific feedback from customers and employees. (You do get this on a weekly basis, don't you?) What issues are cropping up day after day? What are people hearing?

30 Minutes: A Rock, or Single Issue

The big mistake made at weekly meetings is covering everything every week. As a result, the team deals only with issues on a shallow level and never focuses its collective intelligence for a period of time on one issue. The key is focusing on a large priority for the month or quarter, what I described in Chapter 3 as Rocks. Frontline employees spend about ten minutes on this, while the executive team may devote as much as a half hour to it. But, do limit it to just one issue. Attempt more, and nothing will get done. Which issue should be discussed? Choose one of the priorities you've established in your monthly or quarterly meetings, and plan that it should come up for discussion more than once a month or quarter. For example, if one of your priorities is to get an internal information system up and running, the executive with accountability for that project should be in the hot seat at least two or three times over a 13-week quarter, just giving updates and getting feedback. By rotating the topics in this fashion, you'll knock out 15 or 20 rocks each year, you'll do it faster than you thought possible, and you'll feel less brain-dead doing it.

Closing Comments

End your weekly meeting by asking each attendee to sum up with a word or phrase of reaction. It creates a formal closing for the meeting, it ensures that everyone's had a chance to say something, and it gives you a window on what people are thinking and feeling. If you find there are lingering issues or conflicts, you can follow up.

It's ideal if the weekly meeting is just before breakfast, lunch, or happy hour so the executives can have a more informal setting in which to discuss issues that surface during the structured part of the meeting. That informal time is often when real decisions are fleshed out.

The Monthly Meeting—Agenda Is Learning

If the focus of the quarterly and annual meetings is setting strategy and the focus of the daily and weekly meetings is execution, the focus of the monthly is on learning—a chance for the executive team to "pass its DNA" down to the next level. This is a two-hour to four-hour meeting (we take four hours) for the extended management team to gather, to review the progress everyone is making on their priorities, to review the monthly P&L in detail, to discuss what's working and not working from a process standpoint, and to make appropriate adjustments. It's also a time to do an hour or two of specific training.

The key is to involve the entire upper- and middle-management teams, giving them a structured time to work together. This is critical in growing the middle management team and keeping them aligned.

"Why So Many Meetings?

Perhaps you've read this far thinking "We already do these things—either in our quarterly and annual meetings, or one-on-one. We don't need all this extra structure." Let me take one more crack at convincing you, starting with the one-on-one issue.

Daily and weekly meetings are demonstrably superior to one-on-one sessions. In one-on-ones, there's no Greek chorus singing out when the untruths begin to fly. People will give one person excuses that they'd never try before an entire group, where confrontation is likely. Where goals are at stake, and accountability is an issue, the peer pressure of the daily and weekly meetings keeps things moving much better than if an individual exec is reporting to the CEO. Why? Because it's just easier to get the job done than to have to face the team each day, each week, and make the same excuses for having failed to get it done. So, meetings increase the pace of deliverables, and, not incidentally, take lots of time pressure off the leader.

I'm also sold on the value of the collective intelligence that gets harnessed in daily and weekly meetings. Just as the audience lifeline in the television game "Who Wants to Be a Millionaire?" is consistently more accurate than the phone-a-friend lifeline (the equivalent of a one-on-one), getting your entire team's brains focused on an issue is much more effective than focusing one-on-one. A side benefit, of course, is the opportunity these daily and weekly meetings afford you to reinforce your core ideologies and give pats on the back. That's no small advantage.

Sure, you can continue holding your meetings only monthly, quarterly, and annually—forgetting the daily and weekly huddles. If you make your monthly and quarterly meetings more strategically oriented, you'll probably even feel you're doing a wonderful job of keeping up with the breakneck pace of change. But here's my question: as fast as you're pulsing, what makes you so sure you're not headed somewhere you don't want to go? Certainty comes with routine, with rhythm, and yes, with daily and weekly meetings.

Daily Meeting Structure

Focus

Top 1 Bottleneck

Quick Daily Agenda—5 to 15 minutes

2–5 minutes — What's up? Specifics about activities, meetings, accomplishments, noteworthy news from customers, etc.

2–5 minutes — Daily measurements/indicators—from the day before and your goal today.

2–5 minutes — Where are you stuck? Where's the bottleneck? Who's run into a roadblock? What can be done about it? Bite-sized chunks!!

Optional — Review a core ideology.

Stand up, don't sit down, for a meeting.
By phone if only option.

When is your daily meeting going to be? _____

Who is going to attend? _____

Will it be a conference call or stand-up meeting? _____

Whose office? _____

If you need to use a conference bridge, I suggest freeconference.com or rain dance.com. I also recommend using a reminder service like iping.com. At 5:00 p.m. this service calls our cell phones to remind us of our 5:05 p.m. daily call.

Weekly Meeting Structure

Relevancy

Set a time each week to focus on what's important. It may seem impossible at first, but once the habit is created and the meeting is structured properly, most people will look forward to the meeting and find they can't function properly without it. These employee team meetings are *the* major building block for implementing the rest of the ideas you are learning in this book.

To make these meetings productive and useful, I suggest using the following suggested agenda. I also recommend you have the meeting right before a critical time deadline, like lunch or 5:00 p.m. or 8:00 a.m. This will cause the meeting to end on time.

Suggested Agenda

5 minutes—Good News. Go around the group and have everyone share two good news stories, one personal and one business, from the past week. This is a way to counter the negativity of these meetings, since they are mainly focused on addressing challenges, and a way to help people begin to see the good, not just the bad. It's also a great way to get to know each other better and to give each other pats on the back. This may feel awkward at first, but make sure everyone participates.

5 to 10 minutes—The Numbers. Go over everyone's individual or team weekly measures of productivity. Don't get hung up in conversation. Just report the numbers. It's best if the numbers are displayed graphically. It helps people see trends in the data.

10 minutes—Customer and Employee Data. Go over the basic logs. Again, don't get hung up in conversation. Just review whether there are any recurring issues or concerns that the team or its customers are facing day in and day out. Choose one issue and assign a person or small group to explore it to get to the root cause.

10 to 30 minutes—Collective Intelligence. Open the conversation around a rock—a large priority. Use the collective intelligence of the team to drill into a big issue. Have the person with accountability for a rock make a presentation on how they are addressing it.

One-Phrase Closes. Go around the room and let everyone say a word or phrase that represents how they feel at that moment about the meeting.

Keep a Log. Record *who* said they would do *what, when.*

This 30-to-60 minute meeting each week, if effective, will help make everyone's job easier and more productive. If it doesn't, reexamine how the meeting is being run and what is being discussed, but don't quit this crucial rhythm.

9

MASTERING THE BRAND PROMISE

Identify the single most important measurable in building value

Executive summary: What really matters to your customers? What is it that brings your customers to you, and keeps those customers loyally returning, purchase after purchase, year after year? It's your brand promise—the key factor that sets you apart from all competitors. Your brand promise is the starting point from which all other executive decisions are derived. In this chapter, you'll gain valuable tips that will assist you in identifying a brand promise that is both competitive and measurable. Through real-life examples, you'll also see how successful companies evolve and change their brand promise over time. Finally, you'll obtain a tool at the end of this chapter to guide you in determining the brand promise most suited to your vision.

Think back to when Federal Express burst on the scene in the early eighties. What was it that made Fred Smith's new company such a sensation? The answer: It got packages where they were going overnight, no ifs, ands, or buts. Send your package via FedEx and you know your recipient will be holding it by 10:00 a.m. That was Federal Express's come-on to a world that previously knew only the post office. It was FedEx's measurable brand promise.

FedEx's 10:00 a.m. deadline was more than a marketing slogan. It was the key decision that drove all others. To make the promised arrival time, FedEx knows it needs to get its planes out of Memphis by 2:00 a.m. To get the planes in the air on time, FedEx needs me to get my package to the station at Dulles Airport by 10 p.m. Backing up even further on the time line, the FedEx box nearest my home has a 5:15 p.m. pickup time to allow the orange-and-purple truck to complete its route and get to the airport. From the first business plan Smith wrote, and up until quite recently, the company's strategies and tactics existed simply to deliver on this one measurable brand promise. (Nowadays, Smith's delivering on a somewhat different brand promise. More on that later.)

Determining a brand promise is a fateful moment in the life of any company. Choose the right one—the one your customers respond to, the one you can track and execute day after day—and you win. It's that simple. Choose the wrong one and you'll probably flounder for years, never hitting your goals. So how do you choose the right brand promise for your organization?

Start by getting out your One-Page Strategic Plan (yes, again!). Much of what you defined in the Planning Pyramid will serve as a foundation for the following work. Next review your Top 5 and Top 1 of 5 established in Chapter 5. It's quite likely that your brand promise is lurking somewhere in or around these goals. The key worksheet is the Value-Add worksheet found at the end of this chapter. Its five questions will lead you through a thinking process that will help you zero in on your brand promise. But take it one step further—using what I like to call Rockefeller's number-one strategy for maintaining control of your future. Stay tuned.

Consider Your BHAG

Your first point of reference when beginning the search for your measurable brand promise is your BHAG. Remember that Big, Hairy, Audacious Goal? It's where you want to top out in ten years or more. Why ten years? Because it's so far out there, especially in New Economy terms, that nobody can question or debate your aims! This is key to rallying people behind your vision while providing a point of focus that will keep everything aligned. Recall Ronald Reagan's resolve to defeat the Soviet Union's "evil empire." Few bothered to ask how it would be accomplished. They just put their energies behind it and, almost miraculously, it became real.

In business, a BHAG works pretty much the same way. Nike's BHAG was to crush Adidas, which in the seventies seemed plenty hairy and audacious. Starbucks aims to be a bigger brand than Coca-Cola, and who's to say they won't succeed? For Gazelles, our very hairy and audacious goal is to serve 10,000 clients—which would put us among the elite consulting and organizational development firms like McKinsey or Arthur Andersen. Consider this very cool BHAG: founder Jack Stack's BHAG when he started Springfield Remanufacturing (the *Great Game of Business* company that pioneered open-book management) was to have a company where all employees could own their homes and send their children to college.

By the way, all of the BHAGs I've mentioned are measurable. The BHAG serves as the foundational measure against which you determine your brand promise.

Define Your Sandbox

Next, figure out your desired sphere of influence over the next three-to-five years. Are you destined to remain a local company, with customers in one or two cities? Or will you grow to be regional, national, maybe even international? This may not be as obvious a decision as it sounds. And don't assume you can't be a local company and still have some pretty high aspirations, because you can.

When you're done defining your sandbox geographically, take some time to think about your customers and their demographics. Who will you be selling to over the next three to five years? Are there some customers you'll choose to leave to somebody else? Will it take any special techniques to reach your desired customers?

Lastly, consider how many product lines you can logically and reasonably carry. Don't forget to figure out which distribution channels make the most sense for your enterprise. Logistical considerations can make or break your long-range goals. Gazelles' sandbox is delivering organizational development products and services primarily to North American firms with revenues of $5 million to $200 million, and growing at least 20 percent per year. We utilize a direct-sales model and deliver services through local coaches.

Determine Customer Needs

Based on the sandbox you've defined, ask yourself: what is your customers' greatest need? I'm not asking about their wants—they'll "want, want, want" you all the way to bankruptcy if you let them! What you're looking for is what really matters to the customer. At the same time, you want it to be something that demonstrably differentiates you from the competition. At Gazelles, our key customer need is to see action from the knowledge they're receiving. Action is what increases the value or valuation of their firm to their employees, customers and shareholders.

It's at this point you start to align with your BHAG. Nike would have wanted to consider its positioning against Adidas—what does the customer want that he or she can't get from Adidas? Federal Express would consider itself against the post office—how does a customer benefit from choosing FedEx over the local letter carrier? Once you're clear on what that need really is, you'll be that much closer to finding your measurable brand promise.

By way of example, consider the commercial furniture business for a moment. If you've bought a suite of office furniture, you can attest that it's often difficult to tell the difference between one company's brand and those of their three top competitors. So, what's the fundamental need of the customer? If you consider the customer to be the facilities manager who's making the furniture purchase, the fundamental need is to not get yelled at by the CEO and the rest of the executive team. Nobody's going to yell over issues of quality or style. No, what's going to make the executive team read the riot act is a missing part or an installation problem. And, believe it, the manager has enough friends in facilities management to know which furniture company falls short on these key details. The facilities manager is going to go with the company that says, in essence, "we deliver with the least amount of hassle."

Determining customer needs is a tougher task when you've got two sets of customers, as does job-search firm Orion International (see the case study in the Appendix). But, when CEO Jim Tully began working out his company's measurable brand promise, he realized that speed was attractive to both the job candidates Orion deals with and the corporate clients that are Orion's bread and butter. Job candidates want to know that searches and hiring will be completed quickly, and

HR professionals want to rely on Orion to fill their vacancies ASAP. Ideally, Tully needed to find a single brand promise to please both sets of customers, while differentiating himself from his competition. Speed seemed key.

What's Your Measurable Brand Promise?

For Jim Tully at Orion International, the measurable brand promise he hit upon is what he calls "14 Days Done"—whereby Orion will complete a hiring process in two weeks flat, if the client requests it. No other competitor makes such a promise, so it's a potent differentiator in the marketplace. What's more, it's a financially beneficial strategy, because a process that used to take an average of 60 days to complete and be billed now averages 26 days. This shortened cycle time has resulted in better cash flow. It also increased revenues by 78.5 percent within months of implementing "14 Days Done."

However, Tully's brand promise is not only measurable at the end of the placement process. He and his executives quickly realized that their key measurable comes somewhat earlier, in the number of final interviews conducted. That tally gives them a pretty fair guess at how they'll end the month. And they didn't stop measuring there. Tully's team went back over the entire placement cycle, considering each step in the process as a potential moneymaker. They realized that "every step of the way, everything has some value," as Tully puts it.

For a different kind of measurable brand promise, look to Boston Beer, makers of Sam Adams beer. Founder James Koch comes from several generations of brew masters, and his aim and differentiator in the market has always been to make a better-tasting beer—the best, in fact. How does he make that both believable and measurable? By winning major beer competitions. Sam Adams won a consumer-preference poll four years in a row—until the poll was discontinued with that fourth win in 1989. Since then, Sam Adams has competed extraordinarily well in blind taste tests based on style, held at the annual Great American Beer Festival. In 1997, the beer won an unprecedented three gold medals there. What's more, Sam Adams beers have won at least one top honor at the GABF for 14 consecutive years. That gives Boston Beer Company more medal-winning beers than any other craft brewer. Clearly, Boston Beer has earned the right to market its products (of which Sam Adams is but one) as The World's Most Award-Winning Beers.

Bear in mind: your brand promise shouldn't be easily accomplished. It ought to cause some stress in your organization. At Gazelles, our brand promise is 100 percent implementation of the habits deemed crucial to increasing the value of our clients. Not 99 percent, but 100 percent. That's a high standard, and our coaches work hard to deliver. For another lofty brand promise, look to Intuit, makers of the Quicken bookkeeping software for individuals and small businesses. Intuit's initial brand promise was ease of use. To back it up and make it measurable, Intuit promised unlimited support on a $59 piece of software. Clearly, that caused some heart palpitations among designers and managers alike, but it brought out the best in the organization. That unlimited-support promise drove every decision in the company—from how to build the product to how to communicate with customers—so that the customer wouldn't have to call. And, it gave Quicken the solid foothold it needed to get established and grow.

If there is but one warning I can offer you as you home in on your own measurable brand promise, it's to avoid getting caught up in marketing slogans. This is often a point of confusion when huddling to develop a brand promise. Don't get caught up in the wording of a slogan and forget the essence of the exercise. Stay pure. Find the measurable deliverable and leave the sloganeering to the marketing folks. Fred Smith's key decision at FedEx was the promised arrival time. It was up to the marketing firm to convert that advantage into a marketing message.

Control Your Bottleneck or Chokepoint

At last I've arrived at what I like to call Rockefeller's key strategy. Let me pose it to you in a question: Now that you've put a stake in the ground by determining your measurable brand promise, what are you going to do to lock it up, to hold that position? You've got to look for the bottlenecks or chokepoints—there's always one or two—and figure out a strategy to either blow them up or neutralize their threat. For instance, early in the oil business Rockefeller determined that the real shortage in the industry was not oil (it was gushing out of the ground) or refineries (over 1,000 popped up over night), but oak barrels for capturing the oil, and very specifically, the iron rings that hold the oak slats together. So, one of his first acquisitions was a key firm that made the all-important iron rings. Later, when it became clear that transportation costs were the biggest threat to profitability, Rockefeller shifted his energies to that chokepoint.

Let's go back to Intuit and consider Quicken's chokepoint. If you've used bookkeeping software for a while, you know that, in the beginning, one of the trickiest elements of bill paying was lining up the pre-printed checks in the printer. That's true because every printer is—or at least was—a little different. Intuit eventually controlled this bottleneck or chokepoint by having the Quicken standard built into every printer made. Such foresightedness has given Quicken a huge advantage in its burgeoning market. It controlled the chokepoint.

At Boston Beer, founder Koch believes the chokepoint is his hops supply. In fact, he has said that he attributes the honors his beers have won in major competitions to the very select hops he purchases from a special few acres in Bavaria. Not surprisingly, one of the world's largest beer manufacturers once attempted to purchase that acreage, thus locking up the world's supply of these special hops. Luckily, Koch got wind of the attempted purchase, and reasserted his right to them in the nick of time. That, too, is a fine example of controlling your chokepoint.

Are you waiting for me to reveal Gazelles' strategies for controlling chokepoints? Don't hold your breath. If I told you, our competition would know too, right?

Everything Changes—Including Your Brand Promise

Now, if you're an observant consumer, you probably know that Federal Express isn't touting delivery at 10:00 a.m. as a brand promise anymore. Why? Because things change and that includes brand promises.

In many ways, Federal Express lost its brand promise due to its own success. Today, there are many shippers making overnight delivery claims, even the U.S. Postal Service. Delivery by 10:00 a.m. is now merely table stakes. What I mean by that is, you can't even be a player in the shipping business unless you can perform on that once-revolutionary brand promise of overnight delivery. You've got to have those chips in hand to earn your spot at the table.

FedEx's latest brand promise takes it to the next level, which is peace of mind. The measurable deliverable is the customer's ability to know where his or her package is at all times. In other words, what customers want today is tracking. FedEx figured that out several years ago, and quietly spent roughly a billion dollars making sure that customers, big and small, had the necessary terminals installed to handle this new tracking capability. They handed out disks containing the necessary software like so many AOL freebies. Now the brand promise is being sold via the marketing slogan, "Be absolutely sure," and you've probably seen the commercial in which the crocodile hunter keels over from snakebite. Cheerful to the end, the croc hunter acknowledges that the anti-venom was shipped through another carrier, "not Federal Express." Then his eyes roll back in his head and he collapses off-camera.

Please note that Federal Express hasn't stopped guaranteeing delivery at 10:00 a.m.; they've just upped the ante. They deliver early *and* their tracking gives you peace of mind. In a couple of years, it'll probably be early delivery *and* tracking *and*...well, something else, as the previous brand promise becomes mere table stakes. Just like Federal Express's, your once-revolutionary brand promise will someday become table stakes, and probably sooner rather than later. Start working now on the next value-added improvement. If you don't, somebody else will beat you to it.

Your measurable brand promise is crucial. It defines your company in the minds of the public. It gives your organization something huge and galvanizing to strive toward. It does not overstate it one whit to say that your brand promise is a single-minded measure around which all strategic and tactical decisions are made. By considering your BHAG, defining your sandbox, determining customer needs, and controlling your bottleneck or chokepoint, you'll have a measurable brand promise that will set you apart from your competition. That is, until your competition catches up and forces you to up the ante with a new and equally inspiring brand promise.

Value-Add

What is your BHAG?

How do you define your Sandbox—geography, product lines, distribution channels?

What is the biggest "need" your customers have, distinguished from all their "wants"?

What is your measurable Brand Promise?

What is the bottleneck/shortage/chokepoint in your sandbox/industry and how are you going to control it?

What are you going to do to utilize technology?

10

MASTERING THE ART OF BANK FINANCING

Make banks compete to loan you money!

Executive summary: Acquiring financing is a creative process. After reading this chapter, co-authored by the talented Rich Russakoff, you will have a clear understanding of how to effectively work with banks, and you will master the art of shaping the right perception of your business in the banker's (or any other investor's) mind and heart.

> To reach Rich Russakoff, contact Bottom Line Consultants (804-741-5771) or e-mail rich@bottomlineconsultants.com.

An average package and presentation leads to below-average chances of being funded, while a "Knock Your Socks Off" package and presentation will not only get funded, but will often result in:
- Better terms
- Less-restrictive covenants
- Lower interest rates
- Waived fees

These extras can lead to tremendous savings over the life of the loan.

It has been said that the most powerful three-letter word is "ask." You will learn who to ask, how to ask, and what to ask for. This process will show you how to have banks compete against each other to loan you money.

105

Below is a step-by-step process that will take the mystery out of bank financing and show you how to create a thorough, powerful, and compelling document that will put you in the driver's seat. Proper preparation and business savvy will enable you to achieve or surpass your goals.

Step 1:
Loan Opportunity Assessment

The small- to mid-size business market is big business for the banks that have focused on this niche. Bankers are keenly aware of the combined revenues this market generates. It represents a tremendous volume of deposits and fee-producing services, including 401K's, credit cards, direct deposits, letters of credit, and real estate loans, among others.

Equity lending is at a virtual standstill at this time, yet bankers are still looking for good lending opportunities. While the recent downturn in the economy has led to stricter covenants, shorter terms, and more frequent reviews of financial information, the drop in interest rates has made borrowing money from financial institutions cheaper than it has been in years.

Most loans are tied to the prime rate, and interest rates generally vary from prime to prime plus two depending upon the perceived risk of the loan and your ability to negotiate the best possible deal. Unfortunately, the continuing mergers and consolidations of financial institutions have minimized the choices you can seek funding from.

There is no magic involved in acquiring capital. It takes time, hard work, and an understanding of the dynamics of the process. The process consists of three basic phases: Preparation, Presentation, and Persistence.

Let's begin with preparation. You should be aware of the bank's perspective in the loan-assessment process. In essence, there are four levels of risk that banks will weigh:

1. **The transaction itself.** Banks have lending criteria that help them determine whether the loan is a good one for them.
2. **The industry.** Many banks shy away from certain industries. The most commoly shunned include restaurants, construction, gaming, and real estate speculation. If a bank does not understand or

feel comfortable making loans to your industry, you may want to shop elsewhere.

3. **Borrower's financial position.** Lenders will assess not only the health of the business, but your personal financial history as well. I cannot emphasize enough how critical this is. Your character will be judged by your personal credit report. Your business financials should show how you would be able to pay the money back.

4. **Quality of collateral.** How comfortable is the bank with the liquidity of your collateral? In other words, what will your collateral bring in an auction on the courthouse steps during a blizzard in January?

How Much Will You Need?

Your business needs should be your first consideration in determining how much money you seek to finance the growth of your company. Only then should you concern yourself with whether that amount is a realistic target to ask for. Your strategy begins with knowing what your real needs are and then creating a package that a bank (or other investor) would be interested in financing.

If you are purchasing equipment, real estate, or inventory, then you will be able to collateralize the assets you are borrowing. You will also need to determine what percent of the required capital cannot be collateralized and is risky or unrecoverable to the bank (from their perspective).

Because this is a strategic planning process, it will take time, hard work and expertise to determine the right amount for you. Do not hesitate to discuss this in detail with your financial and business advisors.

Growth is another issue to consider. You need to anticipate the costs of growth, including infrastructure. And you need to consider how much growth you are prepared to handle. Consider bringing in a strategic planner and seek the advice of other business owners.

Once you have determined how much money you need, you should consider whether you are prepared to give up equity in your company or incur the necessary debt service required.

In making your decision, you must:

1. Determine what you need.
2. Decide what you're willing to give up.
3. Determine if your opportunity can attract financing, and if not, what you need to do to make it attractive.

4. Be willing to commit whatever time and resources are necessary to achieve your objectives.

By identifying your strengths and weaknesses up front, you will know what you can and cannot expect from a lending institution or any other lending source. How much a bank will lend you will vary from bank to bank. The same is true for the venture capital market and to a host of other financing alternatives.

In short, once you know the right amount to ask for, how much you can acquire depends on who you ask and how you present yourself. Common sense dictates that you borrow or give up no more than you really need to achieve what you want. Any less than what you need can cripple you, and giving up any more than you need to can spell disaster.

Step 2:
Strategy Development

A great loan package and presentation takes considerable planning and may require a team effort. The project will require writing, research, preparing the financials, coordinating appointments, creating graphs, compiling company biographies, making the presentations, and following up with letters, phone calls, and faxes. The project may also require the services of an outside consultant, accountant, or attorney, or all three.

A high-quality package will really stand out, and it will be worth the time, commitment, and cost. You can expect the process to take 40–100 days from start to finish. Allow:

- Three to six weeks for package preparation
- One to three weeks for bank presentations
- Two to four weeks for the bank to process your request, ask for and receive additional information, and generate an offer
- One to three weeks for final paperwork and loan completion

This time frame can easily be extended if there are surprises, such as your needing a life-insurance policy that requires a physical examination that you did not learn about until the day of closing, or holiday or vacation seasons. If your time frame requires quicker turnaround, consider asking for a bridge loan or short-term line of credit.

Many companies wisely decide to turn the loan package preparation and presentation process over to an outside expert because they simply do not have the time or human resources available. Time is money, and in many cases, you need to keep your time and your personnel focused on taking care of business. Even with the best professionals, the process will still demand a great deal of your time.

The Loan Package Is a Strategic Planning Document.

It has been said that the shortest distance between two points is clarity, and strategic planning brings about clarity. Your overall loan package is a strategic plan. A well-written strategic plan spells out what you intend to accomplish and includes both the steps and the resources you need to meet your objectives. A strategic plan extends out at least three years—the current year and the following two. (Five-year plans have little credibility in today's changing marketplace.) Putting together a strategic plan forces you to look beyond today and examine what your company's future needs will be to grow or compete in the marketplace beyond the current year. You will recognize needs for new space, purchasing additional equipment, planning for increased staff or strategic partners, introducing new product lines, or all of the above. Following a strategic planning process allows you to make better decisions because those decisions will take into account your future needs. Over the long term, you will find that you'll hire better, make better purchasing decisions, and make better choices of the markets you decide to enter or leave. Loan officers will be impressed.

I have had the opportunity to observe firsthand the rise and fall of companies that have made it onto the *Inc. 500* list. I discovered that the future-focused companies are the ones that continue to prosper. These companies tend to have a formalized planning process, a detailed marketing plan, and a market intelligence gathering system in place. This pro-active process enables them to take advantage of market trends and opportunities.

If your package and presentation shape the perception that your company is future focused, you may well be halfway home. Not only will your banker see you as a visionary, but you will also find yourself acting like one!

Step 3:
Loan Package Preparation and Research

A great loan package is a selling document. As your ticket of admission to capital, your package should sell and inspire the stakeholders in the business, including you, your bankers, and your employees. The package should make it easy to:

- Understand your future
- Describe where you've come from
- Describe where you are now
- Describe where you are going
- Address potential challenges and strategies
- Outline how you will deal with adversity if you do not reach your stated objectives

As a selling document, your loan package can serve many other important purposes including helping you to negotiate better terms with vendors, assist in recruiting high-quality talent, attract and secure investors, and develop strategic partnerships.

A Knock Your Socks Off Loan Package Will:

- Define your mission or niche in the marketplace
- Present a vision of what the business can accomplish if it is successful
- Demonstrate that you can track your money
- Illustrate how well though out your strategies are and how you are prepared to deal with adversity if it arises
- Outline specifically what you are going to do and how you will accomplish it
- Identify the resources you will need and how you will access the capital to acquire them
- Project where you will be in three to five years and what additional challenges you will face

Bankers are conservative and analytical creatures. The right loan package gives them something tangible to digest and pass on to other key decision makers. In most cases, the loan officer processes the loan applications and makes recommendations to the credit manager and loan committee. It is the loan officer's responsibility to provide the credit manager with the best information he or she possibly can. The right package makes it easier for the loan officer to be your champion to those who have the authority to approve the loan.

The credit manager must make a decision based upon the information you present. His or her focus is generally on crunching your financial numbers to determine if they meet the bank's criteria for lending. The more information you present about the industry, your company, your key management, and your marketing plan, the more likely the credit manager will work with you to find a way to make the numbers work. In short, information can sell your package to people you cannot otherwise reach, people who have the power to say "Yes" or "No."

Most business owners don't present a coherent package for consideration. More often than not, business owners will go to the bank and make their case verbally. They bring in their most recent P&Ls in a form that may do them more harm than good.

Get them everything they need up front. If you can provide a complete Knock your socks off package, the bank will not come back to you for additional information—information that has to be collected, presented, and processed. If you don't, your application will fall off the bank's radar screen, and your loan will get lost in the banker's other day-to-day activities.

It is important to take the attitude that an average package is not a package, it's just average. While substance is critical, sizzle sells. Sizzle includes graphs, charts, research, and articles, as well as the professional look of the package itself. If you take the time to give a banker or investor more in-depth, pertinent information than they expect or are used to seeing, your chances of success are greatly enhanced.

In summary, a complete Knock Your Socks Off package will stand out, and bankers who look at it will see it as something worthy of their consideration. Loan officers have shared with us that a complete, coherent package goes to the top of the pile.

A package should begin with a Table of Contents, which looks like this:

Loan Package Table of Contents
Executive Summary
The Industry
The Company
Management and Ownership
Financial Information/Projections
Purpose of the Loan/Loan Request
Exhibits

Loan Package Examples

Executive Summary Section

Your Executive Summary should create instant excitement and impact. It should spell out your company's mission, clearly state the opportunities you see for your company and industry, and how those opportunities will result in increased earnings and profits. This section should never be more than two or three pages.

Below is an example of the beginning of an Executive Summary from a fictitious computer software company:

> In just five years, XYZ has become one of the largest and most highly respected computer-based training providers within their market niche. XYZ has grown in sales from $805,141 in 1997 to $2,812,322 in 2000, with a 13 percent bottom-line profit.
>
> XYZ projects gross sales in 2001 of close to $4,000,000, with a projected net income of over $700,000. This growth has been completely self-financed, due to XYZ's excellent fiscal management.
>
> XYZ has a strong customer base consisting of companies within the refining, chemical, pulp and paper, power, and pharmaceuticals industries. These industries represent over 15,000 facilities in the United States and Canada.

The challenge in writing the Executive Summary is to avoid rehashing what is inside the package, while immediately creating an interest in the business and opportunity for the bank or investor.

The Industry Section

Never assume the banker knows anything about your industry. It is your job to convey the size, growth, and significance of your industry, as well as your specific niche in the marketplace. Your research should generate quotes from recognized authorities, such as business publications like *Inc.* magazine, *The Wall Street Journal,* and other business publications. Independent research will enhance your credibility.

Below are excerpts from the Industry Section of a loan package for a gaming hall. The owner recognized that he had to convey the size and scope of the industry, as well as its national acceptance, in order to overcome the negatives associated with gambling.

> Last year, Americans wagered about $297.3 billion in casino games and $394 billion in all forms of legal gambling, according to Smith

Barney. That figure has been growing in recent years at about 10 percent annually.

Naomi Talish, an analyst with Morgan Stanley, predicts that the number of riverboat-style casinos and gambling operations, as well as of operations on Indian reservations, is expected to grow rapidly.

The industry has reached the point where casino companies are attracting corporate suitors. An example of this occurred when the ITT Corporation, which operates hotels and casinos internationally through its ITT Sheraton subsidiary, agreed to acquire Caesar's World, Inc. for a reported figure of $1.7 billion.

In three paragraphs, the owner demonstrated not only the size and scope of the industry, but the fact that Wall Street studies the industry and that major corporations are investing heavily in it.

Where to Get the Information You Need:

- Articles from business publications such as *Inc.* magazine and *The Wall Street Journal*
- The Internet and on-line services
- Hire a researcher (maybe an intern)
- Articles about your company
- Citations and recommendation letters
- Research studies
- College libraries
- Robert Morris Associates (a book available at business libraries that provides invaluable industry statistics)
- Corporate annual reports
- SBDC (Small Business Development Center)
- SCORE (Service Corps of Retired Executives)
- Industry associations
- University business professors

The Company Section

In this section, you should show your strengths, as well as your relative position within the marketplace. Below are typical components.

History and Major Accomplishments:
Banks are concerned about your track record. You want to show that you not only have the experience, but also have established yourself in the market. This is the section to boast about your progress.

Divisions, Offices and Shop Locations:
This will clarify the size and scope of your operation.

Market Niche and Competitors:
The more specific you can be about your market niche, the greater credibility you will demonstrate.

You want to clearly show what differentiates you from the competition. It is equally important to identify your major competitors and their market advantages. This information demonstrates that you have done your homework and have a realistic perspective on the marketplace.

Marketing Plan:
The best plans and ideas will not get off the ground if you don't have a fine-tuned marketing plan to drive them. Bankers and investors know that a well-thought-out marketing plan is essential. Your sales and marketing efforts are the fuel that drives the engine.

A good marketing plan includes the methodology you will use to reach your target market. This might include:
- Your data base
- Information-gathering sources
- Who will be doing the marketing
- Specific types of marketing you will be doing
- What the budget will be
- What results you are anticipating
- Why you will get the results you are anticipating
- How you will measure the results
- What you are currently doing and why it is working

Your marketing plan could be a complete section itself.

Clients:
A client list can be impressive because of the diversity of your customer base, the quality and recognizability of the clients, or its sheer size. Even if it is just a list of local businesses, the chances are good that one of them may currently be a client of the bank.

Expansion Plans:

If you are going to use the funds for growth, you should detail your expansion plans and demonstrate that they are both manageable and sound. Remember, while you may be excited about national or global expansion, it might make bankers nervous.

Company Values or Mission Statement:

If you have a Mission Statement or Statement of Company Values, then place it at the beginning of the Company section. Highlighting the statement in italics or a different typeface will set it off nicely.

Profit Centers and Product Lines:

By breaking out your profit centers and product lines one by one, you give the bank a clear understanding of how and where your company makes its money. Do not hesitate to include the gross profit of each profit center, as well as the percentage of business it generates.

Management and Ownership Section

Both bankers and investors will look closely at the quality of personnel who run your company and who will successfully implement your plan. Begin this section with an organizational chart, and then do a brief biography of each of the key people. In the event that you will need to hire additional experts, indicate that need and describe the type of skills you will be looking for.

Do not worry if a key person, including yourself, does not have academic credentials. What is important is to demonstrate the experience and skills they bring to the company.

Here is an example of a Vice President and Chief Operations Officer of a company who has only a high school education, but a wealth of experience.

Mitch Mulch

Vice President and Chief Operations Officer

With Magic Mulch for over 11 years.

Has worked in all areas of the Company:
- Managed the Maintenance Department
- Sales
- Production Manager
- Expertise in equipment management for manufacturing

Promoted to Vice President in 1998.

Currently works with the Mixing/Bagging Department to develop new mixes for customers and has been vital to the development of that Department.

Works in depth with Quality Control and customer materials problems.

Has traveled extensively the last three years to learn about the industry and the competition. Has found more sources for materials at competitive prices and has set up a network of strategic partners across the country.

You should also include a list of your Board of Directors and Advisory Board, as well as the professionals who advise your company, such as your accounting and law firms.

If you are outsourcing key expertise, that should be included as well.

The Financial Information/Projections Section

This will be the most difficult, time-consuming, and challenging aspect of the loan-package creation. Your financial projections should be for a three-year period and be presented through a Best, Probable, and Worst-Case scenario for each year. This should be done on a cash basis, line item by line item, and month by month. It should also include the assumptions that form the basis of these projections and the payback of the loan. This is the best way to show the bank that you really understand the movement and management of cash through your business as well as the strategic financial implications of your goals.

Ideally, your historical financial P&Ls and current balance sheet will indicate top-line and bottom-line growth. If that is not the case, then part of your job is to explain why and indicate how you have corrected (or will correct) the situation. Although it is understandable that you may want to minimize profits or even show a loss on your tax returns, you will need to recast these numbers for the bank so they see the real income the business is generating—discretionary and other.

Items like depreciation, the owner's salary and compensation package, one-time expenses, and discretionary items such as charitable donations, can be added to a recast of the bottom line to add profits or change losses to profits. It will be very effective to chart the recast numbers on a bar graph to accentuate the positive. You will be be required to fill out a personal financial statement with your most recent tax return included.

Your Financial Section Should Include:
- Three-year financial statements (P&Ls)
- Tax returns and recast tax returns
- Personal financial statement
- Aging reports (accounts receivable and accounts payable)
- Balance sheet
- Cash-flow projections
- Projected balance sheet
- Contracts with clients for present and future work
- Information about strategic relationships that will generate business
- Any additional information that will help to make your case

---

The Purpose of the Loan/Loan Request Section

In this section, spell out exactly what you want and reiterate what you will do with the funds. (You did put all this into the executive summary, didn't you?) The section should be short, compelling, and to the point. Here is an example of a company with an unusual request:

The XYZ company is looking for financing tied to purchase orders, as opposed to receivables. Typically, banks are reluctant to loan money tied to purchase orders because the goods or services have not yet been shipped. XYZ is seeking a line of credit of $250,000. The line will be collateralized by purchase orders from XYZ's clients. As described earlier, the client base is made up of Fortune 500 and international companies that manufacture semiconductor equipment.

XYZ is looking for a line of credit to cover the up-front costs involved in purchasing the materials, and the expenses involved in the delivery of these orders.

The value XYZ products offer the market, especially from the standpoint of the ROI of the purchaser, will command a much higher price whenever the perception is that XYZ is a much larger company. The difference in what clients will pay for XYZ's products when the company can offer normal financial terms is up to 25 percent higher.

XYZ's major up-front cost is the purchase of the personal computers that are an integral part of the XYZ package and on which their software operates.

Depending on the size of the order, these computers are purchased immediately upon receipt of a hard copy of the customer's order.

The typical delivery time of the computers is one week, and XYZ must pay for them upon delivery. After the computers arrive, there is generally a two-week turnaround time before shipment is made and an invoice is generated.

Payments are generally received within 45 to 60 days.

The Exhibits Section

This section can include articles written about your company, letters of reference from clients, additional marketing material, citations, awards, pertinent articles about your industry, samples of your contracts from clients and strategic partners, and anything else that will add sizzle to your package.

How the Loan Package Should Look:
- Professionally produced
- Packaged in a three-ring binder with plastic slip for the cover page and professionally printed tabs between sections
- Table of Contents
- Graphics (preferably color) wherever and whenever appropriate
- Appropriate exhibits
- 14-point type
- Block paragraphs
- Numbered pages
- Headers and footers
- Sentences no more than 25 words
- Paragraphs no more than 75 words

Step 4:
Searching for the Right Banks

Taking the time to search for the right bank is critical to a company's long-term success. Whether or not you are currently interested in borrowing from a bank, you always want to establish a working relationship with one that could provide you with all your future needs.

It is a good idea to network with accountants, attorneys, or business peers to identify good banks and loan officers to work with. Ask these referral sources to contact the bank on your behalf and let a bank officer know that they recommend you.

Once you have identified a list of bankers to contact, start with a telephone call. Here is a sample script of how you might approach a banker by phone:

Hi, I'm John Doe, President of XYZ Company in Anytown, USA.

XYZ has been in business since 1987 and develops and markets unique products for the semiconductor industry that improve the efficiency and capacity of the user's products.

XYZ grossed $6,800,000 last year, has already grossed sales of close to $8,000,000 in the first four months, and will probably gross between $20,000,000 and $30,000,000 this year.

Our client market is global, and our niche is in the most growth-oriented segment of the semiconductor industry.

We have an excellent credit history and are looking to establish a long-term relationship with the right bank, which will include a line of credit of between $2,000,000 and $2,500,000 in a working capital loan.

We have prepared a complete loan package that includes historical financial information, and best, worst, and probable financial projections for this year, next year, and the year after, as well as information about our industry and market niche, the management staff, and a history of the company. Would this be the type of client relationship that would interest you?

If they say "Yes," then respond by saying:

Let's set up an appointment for either the 7th, 8th, or 9th of May....
at either 9:00 a.m., 11:30 a.m., or 2:00 p.m.

If they say "No," ask the banker for the name of a loan officer to call whose bank might be interested in your package. Most bankers know which banks can make loans that they cannot. Many business owners have found the right bank through this approach.

There are many reasons why a bank might say "No" on the initial call. For example, the bank might:

- Not lend to businesses in your industry
- Be too conservative
- Perceive you as being too big or too small
- Believe the size of the loan may be inappropriate for their bank
- Not be a business-oriented bank

If, instead, your phone call results in an appointment, ask the banker to bring other decision-makers and to come to your place of business. If your business shows well, a loan officer will get a much better perspective of the dynamics of your company by seeing it in operation. Another reason to ask a banker to come to you is that it requires the banker to make an initial commitment in time, and you will have his or her undivided attention. Bankers love to get out of their offices, and many are required to make at least 20 cold calls per month. Visiting you helps them meet their quota.

Once you go to the trouble of putting together a great package, it only makes sense to identify the best potential lenders and show it to as many of them as possible. The best way to do this effectively is to set up your appointments at your site over a three-day period. A good presentation should last about two to three hours. I like a banker coming in to see another one going out. Bankers are competitive, and if they like the loan, they will work hard to capture your business. Tell each banker you are taking the time to find the right bank for a long-term relationship.

When we assist our clients in obtaining funding, we insist on shopping at least ten banks. Here are ten reasons why:

1. The first two are practice runs.
2. You will fine-tune your presentation with each banker.
3. You will learn different personalities and approaches.
4. You will create a sense of competition and urgency with each banker.
5. You will receive better pricing.
6. You will get better interest rates.

7. You will get better covenants.
8. You will be able to eliminate or minimize bank fees and charges.
9. You will create a buyer's market.
10. You will learn how banks work and bankers think.

This search will put you in the position of being able to pick and choose the right bank for you. Out of the ten banks you interview, ideally there will be at least three who are interested and will provide you with a proposal. The fewer banks you interview, the less opportunity you will have for leverage.

Recently, a high-tech company in New England—one that was experiencing growth of over 50 percent a year, exceeding all its projections, and was extremely profitable—interviewed seven banks. They could only interview seven because there were no more banks in their area. Six of the banks turned them down. They just did not understand or were afraid of the company's industry. The bank that provided them with the loan never knew that they had no competition, and as a result, gave them good terms and covenants, including waiving a personal guarantee. The lesson to be learned here is that there is no way of knowing up front what bank will ultimately provide you with the best overall banking relationship.

Find the Red Flags

Before you make presentations to your target banks, or after you make your first couple of test presentations, you should identify any red flags that might work against you. A red flag is anything that could reflect negatively on your company, including:

- A downturn in your industry
- A poor credit rating
- Increasing accounts payables
- A declining balance sheet
- Ratios that are out of line with industry averages
- New competition

Once these red flags are identified, you should take the initiative in discussing them with your banker, explaining what has occurred and how you are addressing it.

After the interview, if the banker expresses an interest, let them know that you will be reviewing all proposals within two weeks of the last interview. Before you ask for this two-week turnaround, you must be sure to give the bank all they need to move forward. This approach not only creates a sense of competition, but a sense of urgency as well.

If a bank is interested, they will generally provide a written proposal. The proposal will outline the terms and conditions the bank is considering. Proposals, however, are not the same as formal commitments. Most proposals will indicate that they are for discussion purposes only and are subject to a number of considerations. They might include:

- A formal credit approval by the bank
- A review of your most recent financial statements and accounts receivable aging report
- Your agreement to pay out-of-pocket expenses incurred by the bank in connection with any loan documents
- A satisfactory report on a field audit of accounts receivable and your accounting system by a third party who is acceptable to the bank
- Further due diligence deemed necessary and reasonable by the bank

In many cases, the terms and conditions of a commitment letter will be less than what was offered in the proposal. A cynical person might conclude that this is bait-and-switch tactic. Whether it is or not, if you have not interviewed other banks, you will probably be forced to accept less than you should.

An *Inc. 500* company went through this process and received six excellent proposals from various banks. After accepting one of the bank's proposals, they received a commitment letter offering them $300,000 less. Despite the fact that they needed the money immediately, they were so furious that they refused the commitment and called the second bank on their list.

They told the bank what had happened, and said "If you will provide us with a commitment letter today that is the same as your proposal letter, you will be our banker. If not, we will call the next bank on the list." Not only did the bank agree to do the deal, but provided them with a $200,000 bridge loan within 24 hours.

The following graphs are examples of what six banks sent a business owner as their proposal for discussion for a combined line of credit and term loan, and what was actually offered in the commitment letters.

The names of the banks have been changed. In the proposal letter, Unity Bank offered the best overall package. However, when their commitment letter came in, they required a Small Business Administration loan with significant fees. On the other hand, they raised the amount of money they would give as a line of credit from $300,000 to $400,000 and raised the years for the term loan from three to five years. In addition, there were no fees required by the lender by the lender for either loan.

Bank Analysis I: Proposal for Discussion

Bank	Line of Credit					Term Loan				Covenants
	Amount	Terms	Interest	Fee	Calculation	Amount	Terms	Interest	Fee	
1 Unity	$450,000	2 Yrs.	P+1.5%	None	80% - 90 Days	$300,000	7 Yrs.	P+1.75%	None	Rolling 4 quarters cash flow coverage 1.4%; Max debt to worth: 2.0X.
2 Quality	$500,000	1 Yr.	P+1%-2%	1%	75% - 90 Days	$300,000	5 Yrs. +	P+1.5% -2%	None	A/R aging monthly, financials quarterly.
3 Only	$300,000	1 Yr.	P+1%	None	80% - 90 Days	$300,000	3 Yrs.	P+1%	None	To be negotiated.
4 First	$300,000	1 Yr.	P+1%	0.5%	80% - 90 Days	$300,000	7 Yrs.	P+1%	$7500 SBA	Max debt to worth 1.75X; Min net worth $500M; $300M Life assignment
5 Nature's	$500,000	1 Yr.	P+1%	½% Up Front	80% - 90 Days	$150,000	3 Yrs.	P+1.25%	1% Up Front	Max liability to tangible net worth 1.5X; Current ratio 1.25X; Current maturity coverage 1.5X; No dividends or distributions.
6 Hasting's	$400,000	1 Yr.	P+1%	None	80% - 90 Days	$200,000	1 Yr. +	P+1%	None	Min. net worth $500M; Max debt to worth 1.4X; Max owner's comp. $175M; $600M life assignment

Bank Analysis II: Actual Offers

Bank	Line of Credit Amount	Terms	Interest	Fee	Calculation	Term Loan Amount	Terms	Interest	Fee	Covenants
1 Only	$400,000	1 Yr.	P + 1%	None	80% - 90 Days	$300,000	5 Yrs.	P+1%	None	Max debt to worth 2.0X; Min net worth $500M; Cash flow coverage 1.25X.
2 Hasting's	$300,000	1 Yr.	P+1%	None	80% - 90 Days	$300,000	3 Yrs. +	P+1%	None	Min net worth $500M; Max debt to worth 1.4X; $600 Life assignment
3 Quality	$500,000	1 Yr.	P+1.5%	1%	80% - 90 Days	$200,000	3 Yrs.	P+1.5%	None	A/R ages monthly; Financials monthly; Internal Audit Team
4 Unity	$450,000	2 Yrs.	P+1.25%	None	80% - 90 Days	$300,000	7 Yrs.	P+1.5%	SBA 1/2: $3375	Rolling 4 quart. Cash flow coverage 1.4X; Max debt to worth 2.0X.
5 First	$300,000	1 Yr.	P+1%	0.5% Up Front	80% - 90 Days	$300,000	7 Yrs.	P+1.5%	SBA $7500	Max debt to worth 1.75X; Min current ratio 1.25X; Min net worth $500M; $300M life assignment.
6 Nature's	$500,000	1 Yr.	P+1%	½% Up Front	80% - 90 Days	$150,000	3 Yrs.	P+1.25%	1% Up Front	Max liability, tangible net worth 1.5X; Current ratio 1.25X; Current maturity coverage 1.5X; No dividends or Distributions.

John Wooden, the legendary Hall of Fame former coach of UCLA said, "Failing to plan is planning to fail." The difference between giving it your enthusiastic best and reluctantly providing a banker or investor with only the information they request can mean the difference between spectacular success and a disappointing failure. The best way to achieve success in the loan-procurement process is to understand it and to participate actively. Another Hall of Fame coach, Vince Lombardi, once said, "Fatigue makes cowards of us all." If you are willing to understand the process, stay the course, and pay the price, you will create the opportunity to realize your goals and control your destiny.

Keys to Success

- The wisdom to know your strengths and how to highlight them.
- The endurance and patience to go the distance.
- An awareness of your limitations and how to play them down.
- The ability to create the perception that you have the vision, competence, and commitment to execute your plan.
- Demonstrate confidence to the lender.
- Become a master of the system. Be so good at giving the lenders what they want that they are comfortable giving you what you need.
- Be confident and shop until you drop. No one lender knows enough about your business to tell you it can't work.

APPENDIX

Case Studies

Ten firms are highlighted detailing their specific applications of the tools in this book—along with the results they've achieved. And the case studies are rich with marketing, branding, management, and leadership best practices you can apply in your business.

AUTHOR'S NOTE: You will see references to a program called the MBD (Master of Business Dynamics). This was the name given to a series of executive programs my firm Gazelles offers. We no longer use this overarching name, but still offer many of these same executive development programs in which these firms participated—including the two-day "Rockefeller Habits" workshop based on this book. You can view these at www.gazelles.com.

Case study...

CASTEK SOFTWARE FACTORY
Creating Breakthroughs

Like most who've been to the Eureka Ranch, Fay Wu of Castek Software Factory came home to Toronto just itching to put some of Doug Hall's creativity-inspiring ideas to the test. An empty office became the Eureka Room—a place where any of Castek's 160 employees can go to chill and let ideas surface. Intra-departmental problem-solving was thrown out in favor of a full-fledged WOW competition, in which cross-functional teams worked—on their own time—to find solutions to longstanding organizational issues. Is Castek having fun yet? Judge for yourself.

FOUNDED:	1990
PRODUCT/SERVICE:	Component based development (CBD) solutions provider
AVG. GROWTH RATE:	Over 70%
EMPLOYEES:	154

A Room Full of Stimuli

Explains Wu, "Our Eureka Room, which is a takeoff on the Eureka Ranch, looks a lot like a child's playroom. There's bubble furniture, buckets full of candy and colorful paper, stickies, music of all kinds, puzzles, and rolls of paper to draw on. On the walls, we've got colorful slogans about creativity. People who are looking to brainstorm can come in, relax, enjoy the stimuli, listen to a CD, or read an old magazine. These things most likely have nothing to do with what you're doing, but they act as a leaping-off point."

Is It a Hit?

"Well, if I judge by how fast the bubble gum and lollipops disappear, the Eureka Room's being used pretty heavily! Every time I go by I see people sitting there, mapping things out, or just unwinding, which is fine with us. Sometimes whole teams go there, just to let off steam.

The WOW Competition

"We broke the entire organization into teams of about ten people, and each team was asked to tackle a problem relevant to Castek. Each team

brainstormed using the WOW technique, came up with their own definition of the problem they wanted to solve, went away, and, using the
MBD's materials on creativity, came up with a total solution at the end of
a month. The point was to have fun, to practice the Eureka method, and
get solutions to real problems. We found that the teams picked good
problems, and the solutions were of high value to Castek. We've under-
taken to implement as many solutions as possible."

Pretty Pesky Problems

"One team chose to address how we could offer complex systems solutions online, to get as wide a reach as possible. Another team worked on
how to make our Website more appealing, and another team came in
with new names [for software products] instead of acronyms that make
sense to us, but are inscrutable to our audience. There were also teams
that dealt with our biggest issue, growth. One team looked at our space
problem and suggested we combine our Eureka Room with the cafeteria,
and call it the Eurekateria. Another team identified weaknesses in our orientation process. Instead of slowly going through the HR process, they
said, each person should be assigned a mentor, and there should be a fun
day included—maybe including a scavenger hunt to find and meet various people."

Tough Judging

"Each team had a two-hour period to do a presentation, and we were looking for the solutions that really stand out as superb ways of dealing with a
problem. It had to be wicked easy to understand, it had to be magic in how
it all hung together, and it had to be a WOW with the judges. [The pre-
sentations] were all very good. There were skits, videos, each team had its
own song—it was amazing how much talent we found."

And the Winners...

"got things like a day at a big arcade, kickboxing instruction, or, because
this was a creativity competition, puzzles. The first-place team ended up
with surprise trip. A big stretch limo picked them up and took them to a
farm north of the city for an eight-course presentation around locally-
grown and organic food, all prepared by a chef known for his creativity."

Lasting Cultural Change

"Because we used cross-functional teams in our WOW competition, people got to meet lots of people they hadn't met. People have told me

they'd like the opportunity to work in cross-functional teams again. I also think creativity techniques are being used more frequently. Everywhere I go, I see people flap-doodling, and people are less likely to 'kill the new-borns' in meetings. Instead of saying 'no way', it's 'how would you make it work?' Most of all, I think people have been pleased to see the solutions actually implemented. They know the WOW competition wasn't just an academic exercise."

Case study...

EXPRESS-MED
Growing Leaders

Jason Gallourakis, human resources director for Express-Med, uses tools learned at the Master of Business Dynamics' Leadership Challenge Practice with the Tom Peters Company in a 360-degree review process for managers and to give leadership skills to everyone in the organization. Morale is high, commitment to the organization is strong, and a structure is in place that accommodates their phenomenal growth from $1 million in 1995 to more than $30 million in 1999.

FOUNDED:	1994
CEO:	Alan Rudy
PRODUCT/SERVICE:	Mail-order medical supplies
EMPLOYEES:	211
AVG. GROWTH RATE:	164% (COMPOUNDED ANNUAL REVENUE)
WEBSITE:	WWW.EXPRESSMED.COM

Setting up a learning structure

States Gallourakis, "The first group we took through the process back at the company was everybody who was part of the formal, identified management team, but hadn't gone to our MBD meeting in San Francisco. That included 29 people, everybody down to supervisors, along with some others we identified as leaders, despite their titles. Maybe they weren't supervisors, but they were recognized leaders regardless of their position. We took them through a 10-week process using MBD's Deli Zone materials that had sections on Enabling Others to Act, Encouraging the Heart, and the other three leadership principles. Each 90-minute session was led by two co-facilitators who had attended the MBD with Gazelles. One co-facilitator was the person who scored highest in that area or principle; the other was the person who scored lowest—that's something we decided to do while we were still at the MBD."

Self-examination

"Using the LPI software we purchased through Gazelles, we took the management group through all of the skills related to the 360-degree review so they could evaluate themselves, and then let others analyze their skills, too. It created a bond that spanned all levels, because everyone was very upfront with their own scores and weaknesses. It built trust. It gave us a very unified understanding of what we're all working toward. It was culture-building, in a very direct way."

The roll-out

"Over the next 10 to 12 weeks, these leaders took all of our 200 associates through a version of the program teaching the five principles in 60-minute sessions using the MBD's Deli Zone book and tape. People got a diploma at the end, and they loved it. Since then, we've created a class on leadership we've done every six months for new associates."

Opportunities for coaching

"In the beginning, some people thought, why train us for leadership if we're not in management? But once they got into it, people really appreciated the opportunity to evaluate and improve their leadership skills. And they've really enjoyed bouncing ideas off each other. People have looked at their lowest leadership score, then sought out a mentor or coach who has a strong skill set in that area. Then they can get together with their coach and talk about how they handled meetings or situations. Sometimes there'll be general managers taking advice from frontline supervisors, or senior executive team members getting coached by department heads. It's really exciting, of course, to have people above you coming to you for help."

An ongoing structure

"We've actually made the five leadership principles a part of the annual performance appraisal for all leaders. We identify who the leaders are—both the management team leaders and the key leaders in the organization—and we evaluate them with a special form that includes the five leadership principles. At that time we engage in the 360-degree process, and it's very formalized. We also make it a regular practice to tell leadership good-news stories in our newsletters.

Tangible results

"Morale is better, the overall commitment level is higher. We've opened up dialog on issues that hadn't been brought out before. People don't usually feel comfortable criticizing a manager. But the skills we learned through our MBD experience have allowed conversations to occur between levels, without fear, or awkwardness, or tension."

Case study...

HRF EXPLORATION AND PRODUCTION, INC.:
Keeping Partners Happy

HRF, an oil and gas exploration and production company, is not your typical Marketing 1to1 success story. Yet through the Masters of Business Dynamics Marketing 1to1 Practice, they discovered that customer relationship management (CRM) could be successfully applied in a company with a limited number of very large customers. Utilizing Marketing 1to1's IDIC methodology (identify, differentiate, interact, and customize), they raised the professional standards of their employees, deepened trust with their working interest partners, and generated additional revenue for the firm.

FOUNDED:	1993
CEO:	Rick Fruehauf
PRODUCT/SERVICE:	Oil and gas exploration and production
EMPLOYEES:	51

Identify

HRF identified two groups of important relationships: a segment of their 50 working interest partners that required special attention, and employees responsible for recruiting staff for the company's new location in Denver. As they rolled out the program, they also adopted the Disney terminology "bumping the lamp."

The term was coined during the production of one of Disney's animated movies. In one scene a character bumps its head on a street lamp. Disney had a choice of either making the scene a flat two-dimensional animation at low cost or for one million dollars they could cause the lamp to swivel and move all the shadows about. Disney decided they would spend the million to produce the scene in a first-class way. HRF adopted the expression in its company vernacular to mean doing the best you can at the time.

Says CEO Rick Fruehauf, "We started using the expression at HRF to mean going the extra mile and doing the job thoroughly right. We connected it to Marketing 1to1 by treating each customer in a specific way. We improve on what we do, because we are focusing on `bumping the lamp' for them."

Differentiate

A group of working interest partners was differentiated by their need for special attention. Often their requests for information were seen as unnecessary hassles and contentious interactions. HRF considered what was required to make these partners happy and save the company time. "We determined that by spending a few dollars up front, we could reduce requests for information and provide a beneficial service."

Interact

"We began polling the partners by telephone prior to the quarterly meeting to ask what they wanted and expected. We now put on better luncheons when we meet with them quarterly. Rather than using a modest meeting room at a Holiday Inn, we use a country club restaurant. We provide them with more, well-presented data than we have in the past. Instead of 10 loose sheets of paper we provide a bound, professional document for their review. We often give them an industry-related gift such as a paper weight."

Customize

"We keyed in on our partners' body language, noticing when they bristled during our presentation. We noted what caused them to bristle, allowing us to follow up on those issues. We have also improved the quality of our newsletter that goes to all partners. While everyone benefits from it, we focus on this particular group and all the squeaky wheels in general."

"We have also done much more to `bump the lamp' with our employees. As we grow and try to implement our huddles, rocks, and corporate values, the employees who are square pegs in round holes are surfacing. That has required us to look at how we work with these individuals. There are several things that we found we could do: 1. work with some of them one-on-one, 2. move individuals from one supervisor to another, and 3. provide special training. Because they have invested time, energy and resources in our company and we have likewise invested in them, we feel it is important to try to make the employment relationship work."

"We also 'bump the lamp' for new hires by providing them with an agenda covering their first day in the office. We take them to lunch, make the proper introductions through out the company, and expose them to the MBD program, our corporate values, rocks, and goals."

Differentiating Employees

One particular group of employees HRF identified for special attention was the interviewing team responsible for new hires when the company moved a portion of the staff to Denver. "We conducted specific training to prepare them for the interviewing trip. Each team member was given a binder that included the complete agenda, the candidates' resumes, a corporate history, a corporate profile, benefits sketch, and over 100 potential interview questions divided into areas tied to our corporate values."

Results

"The marketing 1-to-1 experience has caused us to be more professional in the day-to-day performance of our jobs, with our working interest partners, employees and new hires."

Case study...

THE LAWRENCE GROUP
Keeping and Growing Customers

Executives at the Lawrence Group, an architecture and interior design firm that knows its clients on a first-name basis, were at first skeptical that Marketing 1to1 had anything to offer them. They only have a handful of customers and customer relationship management (CRM) is at the core of their business. However, at the Master of Business Dynamics Marketing 1to1 workshop, they generated the idea for customer Websites. The sites they created have lead to strengthened client-customer relations, a marketing advantage, and eliminating the need to bid on some client projects. Annual revenue growth in 2000 reached 45% and

The Lawrence Group was rated the best work environment for firms under 250 employees by the *St. Louis Business Journal.*

FOUNDED:	1984
CEO:	Steve Smith
PRODUCT/SERVICE:	Architecture & Interior Design
EMPLOYEES:	119
AVG. GROWTH RATE:	39% (OVER TEN YEARS)

Identify

Marketing 1to1 is a four-step CRM process: identify, differentiate, interact, and customize. The Lawrence Group identified their most valuable customers (MVCs). States CEO Steve Smith, "We have two types of clients. Project-based clients are short-term where we complete one project and after we are done, may get a referral. We also have institutional clients such as hospitals and large corporations that work with us for several years and are our MVCs."

Differentiate

The Lawrence Group differentiated customers by their degree of technical skills, the number of office locations, and the potential for more work. "We had diverse projects with Infinity Broadcasting, a division of CBS, and we knew the client was tech savvy. They have radio facilities around the country and offices in Washington, D.C., San Francisco and Los Angeles as well as regional engineers and other technical people involved in projects. We launched the site during the design phase of the project we built for them in San Francisco."

The customized Websites are accessed through the Lawrence Group home page, giving the general company pages more eyeballs. Clients have a password to access their site that includes a map of the United States with project locations. The Lawrence Group provides all the content for the customized sites and clients gain access to a broad overview of information.

Interact

"On one of our biweekly conference calls, we had the client instructing his people to go to the Website. All us were looking at the same floor plan, costs, project schedule and updates, and executive overviews. This allows all the diverse people to have a snapshot of the project immediately rather than fax or email documents to everyone.

Customers can use our Website as a presentation tool. When the general manager in Los Angeles had a meeting at his location, he invited his local people to our site for his presentation."

Relationship Sticky

"The Website is making relationships sticky. When U.S. West merged with Qwest, we were switched to a different router that could not handle our large document files. When the general manager tried to access the customer Website and could not get in, he delayed the meeting until the site was up and running. We are offering this service as an added benefit and it is amazing how the clients become dependent on the Website.

Our objective is to create stickiness. Not only can we build client facilities but also manage the information. We put cost histories such as electrical costs in various locations on the site. As they use the site, we stay tuned to their additional requests."

Business Strategy

"Our strategy is to treat the customer Websites as a marketing expense. We created a boilerplate of the site so it doesn't cost us as much to create a new one. We have the content. We just need to populate the site with what we already have.

It is internally useful as well. As we load more content, there is more information for us to use. If we are doing a project in another location, we can refer to it for information such as lists of mechanical contractors or the size of the general manager's office."

Eliminated Bids

"Before we created the customer Website for Infinity we really had to stay on the bidding process but now we get projects hands down. We now have three projects simultaneously and the momentum keeps growing for work to come our way.

When we were bidding for one project, we were competing with other firms. When we talked about additional services we offered, they could recognize how valuable this could be. They are a small group of four people who live on airplanes and have to build in multiple markets around the country. Giving them access to information helped them do their job. They got proposals from three firms. We were the highest bid, and they went with us. The decision had to be value driven not price driven.

Expanded Services

Development of the customer Websites has lead to a new division within the company called ReactOne.com. The company has expanded its services beyond the custom Websites to designing entire client sites. "We already knew the clients needs and were in a good position to create other pages for them."

Case study...

LOGICAL CHOICE TECHNOLOGIES
Training Through Tough Times

Logical Choice Technologies hit bottom last year when the company was spending cash on new initiatives just as the market was dropping out from under the computer hardware industry. Amid layoffs and cutbacks, the executive team's first instinct was to pull in and cut out training and development. Rather than do what was intuitive, the CEO, Cynthia Kaye, decided to get around other executives and financial performance experts at the MBD to exchange fresh ideas. The team kept their commitment to training and implemented a set of tools that helped them turn around more quickly, meet their loan covenants, and so impressed their bank that their line of credit was extended.

FOUNDED:	1984
CEO:	Cynthia Kaye
PRODUCT/SERVICE:	Computer Hardware & Services
EMPLOYEES:	60

Tough Times

Growing at 20% per year, Logical Choice Technologies was moving up the Inc. 500 list two years in a row. In early 2000, the company made a decision to spend cash on e-procurement initiatives just as pricing pressure was heating up. Bottom line was everything in the corporate world. The public sector was no different and the state of Georgia issued its first freeze. SG & A was increasing faster than sales.

Drastic Changes

The severity of the situation became evident when Cynthia Kaye and half the employees returned from a prepaid trip to Mexico. Says Kaye, "I came back tanned and relaxed, and the COO, who had stayed behind, looked white as a ghost. He said if the company kept going as it was, we would be out of business in a couple of months. I thought he was exaggerating. We pulled out the numbers and sure enough, we were not going to make our loan covenants if we didn't make drastic changes." Matters became worse entering the fall as the equity market changed rapidly and the company faced not making payroll. "We had to come together as a management team, make hard decisions, and lay off eight or nine people."

Creative Solutions

The company was in survival mode and chose to get creative. Through layoffs and a stock for salary exchange plan, the company was able to reduce monthly SG & A by $100,000. Some employees took a second mortgage on the their house, and others did not take a paycheck for two months in order to help keep the company going.

New Tools

At this pivotal point, the executive team was scheduled to attend the MBD's Great Game of Business (GGOB) workshop. "I don't know what would have happened if we had not gone to GGOB. We could have stayed home and spent two days talking to each other but getting out and talking to some of the other business folks at the workshop kept challenging us to think out of our box. With all the stimulation going on we were able to come up with new ideas."

4' by 8' White Boards

When the team returned from the workshop, they began implementing the key tools immediately. "Giving everyone the GGOB book and the cassette tape to get a little bit of buy in and to understand the smart numbers worked well." The next step was to create a war room, figure out the three smart numbers and the critical number. They moved people out of an office, drilled seven sheets of 4' by 8' white board at $10 each into the wall, and made their own conference table out of a sheet of wood. The white boards are used to track three smart numbers and a critical number and compensation is tied directly to gross profit.

Everybody Matters

By using the white boards and games, the employees have become a lot more cognizant of what happens to numbers. There is a greater appreciation for working through a problem and knowing each individuals contribution to the big picture. "When the checks come in the mail, the sooner the receptionist gets them to the bank the more interest earned. She understands that every dollar makes a difference and is now excited about running to the bank. That helps morale."

Debt to Equity Ratio

Executives meet weekly in the war room to review the numbers. Department heads also meet there around their own critical numbers and charts. Debt to equity ratio takes up a whole board and that number has come down from 7 to 1 to 4 to 1. The current goal is to get it to 3 to 1. "At the end of the month we go into the details of how and why the numbers went up or down. It is a good learning experience."

Lenders Visit

"The lenders visited our war room which is typically only used for internal office meetings and were very impressed with our discipline. We made some sacrifices and changes and are moving in the right direction. They believe in us and have increased our line of credit. While we are not running by the seat of our pants, hoping things will work out, we aren't out of the woods yet. We have to keep pace with the training and always grow ourselves."

Case study…

MARLO FURNITURE
Alignment Drives Performance

Marlo Furniture applies the Master of Business Dynamics' Great Game of Business Practice scoreboards and forecasting tools throughout their stores. In six months, they reduced non-sales staff and payroll 20 percent, while revenues increased and managerial staff turnover dropped from 30% to 2%. In addition, inventory turns increased and the number of customers who would refer Marlo's to a friend increased from 80% to nearly 100%.

FOUNDED:	1955
PRESIDENT:	Neal Glickfield
PRODUCT/SERVICE:	Largest furniture store in metropolitan Washington, D.C.
EMPLOYEES:	500
WEBSITE:	WWW.MARLOFURNITURE.COM

Know and teach the rules

Every quarter, the company closes the stores and hosts an all-employee, half-day training program for their 500 associates. A slideshow is presented with the company vision, the "five big rocks," last quarter's achievements and next quarter's plans. Similar to an in-house trade show, managers have booths for employees to learn more about each division and its critical number and how the business is run.

Weekly huddles

Spearheading the success at Marlo's is the forecasting and scorekeeping at their weekly huddles. Managers track critical numbers on large whiteboards installed in all the stores' meeting rooms. Upon arriving at the weekly meeting, they write their critical numbers on the board. After a round of good news stories, the team looks at every line item to check the actual numbers against those predicted. Significant variances are reviewed and solutions are created to head off any downturns in productivity. Once the numbers are discussed, a new round of forecasting next week's numbers begins.

Critical numbers

An important part of the huddle is coming to agreement on what the critical number should be. Company-wide critical numbers are established as well as goals for each division. Whether it's the number of items in stock at the time of order or the number of customer returns, once it is decided, they start measuring it. One quarter this year, in order to improve customer satisfaction and increase sales, the critical number was the percent of customers who would refer Marlo's to a friend.

The management team established the baseline of referrals at 80%. As they followed the number during the quarter, it rose to 90%. The focus for the third month was turning the remaining 10% around. Employees would survey customers at the point of delivery and try to handle any problems that occurred. If they could not solve the problem on the spot, they would turn it over to management. Employees were able to turn around half of the dissatisfied customers and closed the quarter with customer referrals at 95%.

Profitable habits

Driving a number creates profitable habits. Once they focus on a number for a quarter it tends to stay favorable allowing Marlo's to focus on another part of the business that builds their success. "We have built on every preceding critical number as a piece of a bigger picture. We start simple and then make it more complex. We're still watching other numbers, if something goes astray we will bring it back in." The number of customers who would refer Marlo's to a friend reached 100% this quarter.

Stake in the Action

Quarterly bonuses build incentive into the process. Employees receive 100% of the bonus if the company number and division numbers are met. The bonus pays out at 50% if the division makes its number and the company does not. Only employees with perfect attendance at training programs and satisfactory performance reviews, are eligible for the bonus, further encouraging positive habits. The company runs more smoothly by measuring critical numbers, sharing the numbers with all employees, and meeting regularly around the scoreboards. Marlo's has reduced sales staff and payroll while increasing revenue. Employee moral is up as measured by the decrease in managerial staff turnover from 30% to 2%. Identifying problem areas and resolving them quickly makes for a spirited workplace and more profitable company.

Case study...

MCKINNEY LUMBER
Increasing Productivity and Retention

McKinney Lumber is a 400-person pallet manufacturing company in an industry with wild price fluctuations and 50 percent average employee turnover. By implementing Great Game of Business tools from the MBD, the executive team engaged the frontline in measuring productivity levels of everyone in the company. They began training all the employees in business fundamentals one hour a week in a converted warehouse. Building knowledge deep into the organization transformed the company's culture and raised retention levels to the mid-80 percentile while maintaining an average growth rate of 25%. In addition, today employees know precisely how they are doing every day.

FOUNDED:	1953
CEO:	Joe McKinney
PRODUCT/SERVICE:	Manufacture industrial lumber and pallets
EMPLOYEES:	400
AVG. GROWTH RATE:	25% PER YEAR FOR 25 YEARS

Training the Entire Organization

Says CEO McKinney, "We started by training the upper management group, but the more we did, the more we realized we needed to teach the entire organization in order for people to understand. The decisions we were asking people to make on bottom-line issues were contrary to the beliefs of the average line worker. Employees really believed that 'the man is trying to keep me down,' and that we had all the money in the world."

85% Profit?

"When I asked these people what portion of every dollar of sales I keep as profit, even my office staff—who sees the checks and invoices—got it wrong. The low answer was 15 cents, and the high was 85. I actually retain less than 5 percent. So I started having lunchtime meetings to discuss these things."

We Can't Afford Lunch Anymore

"Early on I asked them, if we wasted $100, how many dollars in sales would it take to offset that $100? At a 2 percent profit, it's $5,000. And I knew employees were starting to get it when one of them asked me how many dollars in sales it had cost to provide lunch that day. If I remember correctly, we had a $19,000 lunch. And you know what the employee said? 'We can't afford lunch anymore.'"

Learning by Selling Sandwiches

"Inspired by the MBD DeliZone, we started a McSandwich business to teach about the balance sheet, income, and cash flow statements. First we got investors. I put in $5, and others did, and we borrowed from 'the bank' to get started. I went to the grocery store and bought bologna, cheese, bread, mayo, and mustard. Then we had a balance sheet. The bread and other things were inventory, we had some cash, and we had equity because we had investors, and because we owed the bank, we had liabilities.

"We began selling sandwiches at our lunchtime meetings. We noticed that bologna was costing us 20 cents per slice, bread cost something else, and soon we could see our cost of goods sold. We hired upper managers to make sandwiches, so we had labor costs. We also rented space. All these things changed our cost of goods sold. Every time we sold a sandwich we reduced our inventory and showed that on a balance sheet. Each week we could tell if we'd made money or did not. We carried that across to a cash flow statement."

Out of Business

"One week we offered credit, and that meant our accounts receivable went up, but there was no cash, so guess what? We didn't have enough money to buy bologna. We'd made a profit, but we were out of business. The bank came to the rescue, but then we needed to pay on the loan every week. We kept it up until people had a flow for what was happening. It was the best thing we could have done to show there is no way to hide money in a balance sheet. You can move it, but there's always a day of reckoning."

Creating Employee Buy-in

"When we established functional teams, our goal was to get them to understand that what we were trying to do long-term was to know how the company was doing every week, profit or loss. I started by asking the teams to find something in their area to measure. So each team chose its own measurement. You would have laughed at some of them. The numbers were worthless, but that wasn't the point. We were measuring. Then we asked, if your number went up, did you have a better week or a worse week? Over time they realized that their measurements weren't good ones, and they changed them."

Watching Costs

"Now we have employees watching four basic cost lines that create our cost per unit. Overall, they're looking at units per time and cost per unit. They know what their planned production is, units per time and also what the planned unit cost is. Every week they report a dollar variance for the week, up or down, from plan. And we're working on a reward system for it now."

Correcting Weaknesses and Rewarding Employees

"Every time you make improvements, you expose your weaknesses, and as you expose your weaknesses, you discover where you need improvements. We're at a point now that we're finding structural weaknesses. We have people, positions, and responsibilities overlapping, and we need to restructure. We're also trying to put in place a parallel system for employee and executive compensation."

Case study...

MOSTLY MUFFINS
Ingredients for Tripling Profitability and Doubling Cash

Developing as a leader has helped Molly Bolanos meet the challenges of growing a baked goods company from scratch to $10 million, tripling profitability and doubling cash. The bigger the company has grown, the more important it's become to streamline data analysis down from monthly reports to daily numbers. In less than an hour every morning, information cascades throughout the entire company, simplifying management and allowing more time for focusing on growing the business.

FOUNDED:	1987
CEO:	Molly Bolanos
PRODUCT/SERVICE:	Baked Goods
EMPLOYEES:	100
ANNUAL REVENUE:	$10 MILLION

Starting from Scratch

Molly and her childhood friend Anne Marie Flaherty rented a local school kitchen and began providing baked goods to coffee vendors at the age of 21. From their initial investment of $1800, the company has grown to $10 million in annual revenue and expanded into coffee houses, airports, ferry terminals, and grocery stores.

Commitment to Training

Molly's personal commitment to training has helped her and the company over the pitfalls of organizational growth. "Every stage of development has had its own set of issues," says Bolanos, "I understood intellectually what needed to happen to run a company, but doing the things that you read about has been the biggest challenge. Rather than just react in the middle of a crisis, the MBD has helped me forecast and prepare for what's ahead."

Becoming a Leader

Learning how to delegate and let other people be the hero was Molly's biggest challenge in going from $1 million to $5 million. "Working with Gazelles and the MBD coach has helped me be the predictor and not the doer. When we were at $1 million in revenue, I was the sales rep, production manager, delivery driver, and customer service rep. Emotionally and intellectually I needed to have control. Unless I stopped doing these things, I was a roadblock in the company. Through the MBD I have had the opportunity to learn from others who are growing their business and remain significant in their company by providing leadership. My leadership ability is to connect to my staff and vendors and to promote the company and where we are going."

Growing Customers

Adding to the ongoing training, Molly learned in the MBD Marketing 1to1 workshop that all customer relationships are not the same. "I ranked every single customer in five key areas, such as how well they pay, how well they display our product, and how well they represent us. For our second quarter theme, we took our most valuable customers and created targeted merchandise programs. Within a week, we had over a million dollars in proposals out to several large companies." The customized approach to up selling eliminated the need to create a new product line and resulted in more money for the company and its customers.

Meeting Rhythm

Daily, weekly, and monthly meetings and tracking critical numbers has increased the ability of the management team to manage the business more efficiently. Information flows through the company in a series of daily morning meetings. The executive team meets for a 15-minute huddle to review five major numbers, the top one of the five and any roadblocks. The production team meets at 9:00, followed by an office team meeting at 9:30.

Daily huddles are the communication link in the company, creating alignment, building team spirit, and reducing response time. "Everyone knows from the meetings what the critical numbers are. Two years ago, when we had monthly financials done out of house, it would be six to seven weeks before we looked at the numbers. Now, if we blow it in production, it shows up the next day."

Measures and Data

Daily bench marking and key result indicators reveal cash, units, and pounds per man hours. These numbers are trended weekly. "It was a huge transition from running a company based on gut feeling and walking around to having measures and data. I am no longer managing the income statement. We are managing our gross margins and deficits. If a number is too high or too low we can manage the variance."

Managing Forward

Executives spend a half hour a week looking at trends in the critical numbers and a half day a month is set aside to hit all the roadblocks, strategize and plan for what's ahead. Quarterly themes overlay the meeting rhythm to pull everyone together around a critical number. "The whole process has everyone focused and keeps it fun. People get excited by keeping their eyes up and out, instead of down. Knowing we are going to the next level helps us manage in a downturn.

Infinite Potential

As the food industry moves towards more organic products, the company is keeping pace by launching a new product line. The only bakery in the Northwest certified organic, Mostly Muffins will roll out the new product along side Starbucks organic coffee. "We blinked and got to $10 million. The next stage is to get to $30 million. The questions I ask myself are, who do I have to be and what do I have to do to get there?" asks Bolanos.

Case study...

ORION INTERNATIONAL
Gaining a Market Advantage

A company's brand promise is a guaranteed outcome that matches the key need of its customers while differentiating it from the competition. Orion, an executive placement service, established a measurable brand promise with its premier service of "14 Days Done." Since adding the service to its mix five months ago, Orion has reduced it's average placement cycle by 65 percent, from 40 days to 26 in an industry with 60-day averages. Over this same time period, the brand promise has become a cash accelerator, provided Orion a market advantage and company focus, and led to a 78.5% increase in revenue in 2000.

FOUNDED:	1991
CEO:	Jim Tully
Product/Service:	Customized hiring solutions
Employees:	204
Average Growth Annual:	78.5% (projected 2000)
WEBSITE:	WWW.ORIONINTERNATIONAL.COM

Customer Focused

Orion developed their brand promise with the help of the Master of Business Dynamics Planning Pyramid Organizer. The promise focuses on the two sides of their business that add up to cash revenue—finding qualified candidates and identifying the needs of clients. For both parties time is critical and a key differentiator. For candidates, knowing a client wants to complete the hire in 14 days, indicates a serious opportunity. For the clients, knowing Orion could fill a position quickly if needed provides peace of mind.

Cash is King

What is good for the customer is also good for Orion. The longer the interview process, the longer to close the sale, which negatively impacts the business. Says CEO Tully, "We measured all the time lines and found ourselves with a 60-day cycle from the time of the job order to the day we invoice. If we could shorten this cycle time, it would be the single best cash item, and cash is king."

Innovative Approach

Orion created a mini-conference as an earlier initiative for reducing cycle time. They collapsed the traditional step of interviewing candidates into one day. "We would go to a client site on a specific date that they designated and bring in qualified applicants for the position. Companies liked it. Once we knew their profile and process, they could do one hiring event."

Branding

The challenge was figuring out how to replicate the process on a macro scale with all their clients. "Time was the biggest bad guy. Stuff happens, other interviews come up. The deal isn't done until you get the offer made and accepted." By creating the premier service of "14 Days Done," Orion used time as a marketing tool and advantage and to bring focus to what can be a messy process.

"The brand promise helped clean up both sides of our business. It eliminated the bottlenecks and surprises ordinarily faced in the industry. We could more quickly identify the needs of our clients and candidates. Just the fact that our 14 day brand promise is out there, gets clients off the dime. It let's people know how fast it can work, how we can solve problems if companies want to move fast."

Roll Out

"We announced the brand promise of 14 Days Done at 14:14 hours on the 14th of April. I made a nationwide announcement to all the employees. We had them call into a conference number and I announced the brand promise to everyone from my desk. I couldn't read their faces because I couldn't see them. But I could hear the voices from down the hall and they were getting excited."

"We gave everyone shirts and hats with the promise printed on them. All the regional managers were given a desk clock with two mechanical gears that would flip the hands every fifteen seconds. One side of the hands says Orion, and the other side says 14 Days Done. When there are great stories about 14 day successes, we print them on bronze coin medallions to give to employees."

Going Deeper

Orion has taken the process further by measuring every step. "The number of final interviews became the measurable number for knowing how we would do by the end of a month or quarter. We could always speculate, but by looking at it carefully we established a monetary value for each stage of an interview. We began to not just see value at the end the hiring process. Every step of the way, everything has some value."

Results

Since instituting the brand promise of 14 Days Done, revenues have increased 78.5% and the average cycle time has been reduced by 65%, from 40 days to 26. "It has made a significant impact in driving cycle time down because everyone is aware of it as a critical number."

Case study...

THE SCOOTER STORE
Managing Hyper Growth

Increasing revenue by 287% over the last 9 months while growing from 163 employees to 441 in the same time period, The SCOOTER Store is managing hyper growth by applying the fundamental habits of the Master of Business Dynamics. By training the entire organization, using regular meetings to create alignment, and tracking hassles, work is focused, efficient and fun. Two of the reasons for soaring revenues are the 150% increase in the average sales volume for mobility consultants and an employee retention rate of 97.3%.

FOUNDED: 1991
CEO: Doug Harrison
PRODUCT/SERVICE: Power chairs and scooters, accessories, automobile lifts
EMPLOYEES: 441
AVG. GROWTH RATE: 287% (over nine months)
WEBSITE: WWW.SCOOTERSTORE.COM

Education Delivered Throughout Organization

After the Senior Management Team attends a MBD Practice, the information is delivered throughout the company by Rich LaHaye, VP of PeopleWerks!, the Human Resources Division of The SCOOTER Store. Monthly manager meetings offer Rich the ideal structure to train mid-level managers in the Practices. He provides them with tools, such as videos and handouts and an example of how to deliver the message to their employees, emphasizing "practicing what you preach." Managers and employees eagerly await the next level of Practice.

New Employee Training

The SCOOTER Store has incorporated the MBD tools company-wide into every aspect of Human Resources and training. Both the Leadership Challenge and Masters of Business Dynamics "Bridging the Gap" are offered as regular training to new employees. Managers occasionally send employees through the course a second time for a refresher.

Making it Visible

The SCOOTER Store utilizes the MBD materials in training sessions and the classes receive high employee satisfaction ratings. Rich has memorialized the MBD tools in simple ways such as posters throughout the company as well as colorful flyers. You can spot them throughout many of The SCOOTER Store locations.

Regular Monthly Meetings

The SCOOTER Store hosts monthly manager meetings at a variety of locations lasting anywhere from six hours to a full weekend. At the February 2000 meeting, they focused on the MBD Planning Pyramid where they broke into groups and focused on planning for the individual departments. Emphasis was placed on 'measures' and how you can't master what you can't measure.

Weekly and Daily Huddles

Company-wide, each department holds a weekly meeting and daily morning huddles. Weekly meeting times and days vary according to the preference of each department. These weekly meetings are a time for good news stories and review of measurements and hassles.

Hassle Cards Improve Operations

To implement another MBD habit, Rich created hassle cards and had them color-coded for each department. The cards are available to all employees and they are encouraged to fill them out and present them at their weekly meetings.

The Training Coordinator receives the hassle/suggestion cards, logs the information and then passes it along to the appropriate manager for resolution. Employee use of this easy access system to make suggestions and voice concerns is creating improvements in all areas of the company. The SCOOTER Store is creating an electronic hassle/suggestion card that employees can easily access through their Intranet.

Creating Positive Changes

When the roll out of hassle cards began—there were a few moans and groans, but once folks got the idea of how much they could and would change things for the better, they began to roll in. Tim Zipp, Vice President of Reimbursement, required all employees to hand in a hassle card as an admittance ticket to the weekly meeting. Employees had to have one even if they said they had no hassle. This got employees in the habit of using them and led to positive changes in the company.